You Had Me at Re: Hello

The Ultimate Guide to Online Dating, Including Tips & Testimonies

Original Edition

SAGE WILCOX

You Had Me at Re: Hello
The Ultimate Guide to Online Dating, Including Tips and
Testimonies

First Edition, 2016

ISBN-13: 978-1-945290-10-7

ISBN-10: 1-945290-10-2

Library of Congress Control Number: 2016959886

Printed in the United States of America.

DEDICATION/ACKNOWLEDGMENTS

This is dedicated to all of the people who are working hard to better their situations, day by day, and in every way. Perseverance and discipline pays off. YOU deserve to make your dreams come true and reach your full potential, and this book is for you. Enjoy!

Deep, humble appreciation to the Divine Source, whom I aspire to grow closer to every day, in faith.

Thanks to all who made this book possible. Also to those who loved and supported me as I worked on getting it published. You know who you are, and I am so appreciative and grateful.

Sincere gratitude goes to those who submitted their online dating testimonies. It takes courage to share our personal stories but it is in sharing that we are able to reach out and help others who are going through similar situations. People can relate easier to those who are real and sincere. We can all learn from each other - there is beauty in this knowledge.

And last but not least, to the readers. Thank you for taking the time to read this book. I hope you enjoy it and find something inside that resonates and inspires you in some way. Thank you. Let's pour our favorite drink, find a comfortable spot, and get started, shall we? Our dreams and goals are waiting to be fulfilled.

Other books by Sage Wilcox:

- *Love Letters from Exes: Proof That Life Goes On After a Break Up and Love Is What You Make It*

- *Get It Up: 101 Ways to Raise Your Vibration, Reduce Stress, Depression, & Anxiety, Increase Joy, Peace, & Happiness and Attract Abundance Automatically!*

- *The 2-Hour Vacation: Let Go and Relax, Reduce Stress & Anxiety, Gain Inner Peace, and Happiness*

- *Until We Fall (A Romance Novel)*

- *The Importance of Doing It: How to Utilize Discipline to Get Out of Bed, and Make Your Dreams Come True! A Guide to Taking Action to Create Successful Habits, Reduce Stress, Anxiety, & Depression & Gain Self-Discipline, Motivation, & Success!*

- *Less Is Best: Declutter, Organize, & Simplify to Reach Minimalism; Get More Time, Money, & Energy*

Please visit her website at:
http://sagewilcox.wix.com/books

CONTENTS

INTRODUCTION

"In my dreams, I could be a Princess, and that's what I was. Like most little girls, I believed nothing less than a Prince could make my dreams come true." ~ Loretta Young

---

One of the things that make online dating so popular is the fantasy we build in our head about finding the right one or finding our Prince Charming.

In 2005, not many Americans had a lot of experience when it came to dating online. The Pew Research Center* conducted a poll at that time asking people across the United States what they knew about it. Many didn't have much exposure to online dating or to people who used it, and a lot of people saw it as an inferior way to meet someone.

Nowadays, nearly half of Americans know someone who is using dating sites or who has met a mate through online dating. What's more, our attitudes about online dating have become a lot more positive. In only three years, the number of 18-24-year-olds who use dating sites has almost tripled from 10% in 2013 up to 27%. The number of those online dating in the 55-64-year-old bracket has also doubled from 6% in 2013 to 12% today.

The surge of millennials using online dating is in part due to mobile apps – around one in five 18-24-year-olds (22%) now use mobile dating apps, just three years ago, only five percent did.

Despite the rapid growth of online daters, one-third of online daters report that they haven't yet met up in real life with someone they met on a dating site. In fact, although one in ten Americans are using online dating, most relationships still begin offline. Nevertheless, online dating is on the rise and it's only going to become more popular in the future.

Are you interested in online dating? We're going to cover what you need to know (no-holds-bar!), the pros and cons of meeting someone online, online dating etiquette dos and don'ts, how to spot a scammer, and most importantly, how to stay safe.

The ideas in this book are merely suggestions based on observations and data. It is meant to challenge you into getting out from under the weight of misconception and to see things as close as possible to what they really are.

A few of these suggestions are based on a perspective that is not mainstream at the moment and so may seem a little alien to some, but will make complete sense to others, and make sense to dissenters with deeper thought.

It has been a long tradition in the minds of our generation's youth, that marriage is the fruit of love. The ancients have always said otherwise. And the next generation has been looking at the subject of marriage then turn out to be a never ending debate that raged between the romantic and the realist. Both are true in their perspectives, as things often occupy the juxtaposition between the two.

The ancients who vociferously exalted the virtues of

arranged marriages knew one thing to be true: that all marriages are not bound by just the concept of love but the strength of the resolve. The decision to get married is secondary to the decision to stay married. In this regard, how one meets, whether it's at the altar as the natural progression of an arranged marriage, after courting for years and falling in love, or by meeting online and taking it one step at a time. The method of how one gets there are many, but the promise is one and the same.

Those who are interested in online dating should know that the chances of finding a meaningful relationship can be slim, and the chance of losing hope is real. Hope is the motivation that gets you back on your feet in the event of a failed attempt at a relationship. Online dating, in all reality, is just a way to meet new people and socialize. If you look at it that way, then it's no different than signing up for a social media account. Except that with online dating, things may obviously go a little further.

Online dating has commoditized one of our basic purposes and pleasures in life by categorizing and putting together databases across the world of people who we could possibly create a life with. But in earnest, it's also a list of people who we could actually just become friends with.

Online dating as a tool to meet new people is great, as long as you take the necessary precautions and stay vigilant. As a tool to seek marriage, it might not be as effective. But be prepared to objectify and be objectified. That is the social contract of all those who sign up, because when you do, you agree to be taken superficially just as you look at others and you subject yourself to their judgments as you pronounce yours on them.

Regardless of what you believe a marriage should look like,

how you look at dating, especially online dating, should not be affected. Because marriage is a decision, not a fleeting sense of euphoria. It is a conscious attempt on one hand and is a complete mutual surrender on the other. But all this begins at the point of marriage. How we get to this point is not important as long as the actions taken don't effectively spill over into the institution of marriage.

In past cultures, marriage was arranged by the parents and the guardians. They would arrange marriages based on an array of factors including family status and potential earning capacity. In eastern cultures, this was complicated by class and caste systems. In the west, marriages were the result of political and financial unions for the upper classes, and for the regular folk, it was essentially someone within your own town.

Today, our collective reach has increased, we travel to other states for school, we go overseas for work, foreign cultures come here and there is a lot of mingling at the international level that exposes us to more opportunities than we had just half a century ago.

Today we have more than 52 million people who are single in the United States. We have almost 50 million people who have tried online dating. The thing to note here is that not all of those who try online dating are single, just in case you are inclined to look at those numbers and think that almost 100% of those who are single have tried online dating. Not cool, I know, but the fact remains, it happens. There are many people on these dating sites who are not single.

The online dating industry is fairly large in the sense that it covers a large number of singles and non-singles. In fact, last year the industry is approximated to have generated over $1.7 billion in revenue. If you remove the outliers in the survey, and focus in on only those that were fairly serious about dating online, you will find that the average they spent was over $200 per year on dating sites.

As a business, it's easy to see that this is a growing industry. But there are two sides to the counter opinion. There are those who oppose the idea of having to meet a future spouse via an online dating site; and there are those who see it as a more effective way to increase the sampling rate, thereby increasing the probability for success.

Whichever way you see it; online dating is not about the post-wedding state as much as you may be inclined to think. Online dating, today, has evolved into being more about a social experience than a prelude to building a family. Some supporters of the online dating culture are vociferous that the best way to go about finding your best partner is by playing the odds - the more people you come across and meet, the higher the chance that you will find the right person.

Many people do find their mates through online dating, and we are going to give you all the information you need to decide if it's right for you or someone you know.

*http://www.pewresearch.org/fact-tank/2016/02/29/5-facts-about-online-dating/

1.
ONLINE DATING FACTS AND FIGURES

Here are some more facts and figures that will help you understand the wild world of online dating:

How Many People Are Online Dating?

1. *Number of people in the US who are single: 54,250,000*

2. *Number of people in the US who have tried online dating: 49,250,000*

3. *Number of members on eHarmony: 16,500,000*

4. *Number of members on Match.com: 23,575,000*

What is the World of Online Dating Like? Ten Facts:

1. *Money spent on online dating per year: $1,749,000,000*

2. *Money spent by a dating site member per year:*

$243

3. *Length of courtship for married couples that met online: 18.5 Months*

4. *Length of courtship for married couples that met offline: 42 months*

5. *Number of users who left an online dating site within the first three months: 10%*

6. *Number of male online daters: 52.4%*

7. *Number of female online daters: 47.6%*

8. *Currently committed relationships where the couple met online: 20% of all*

9. *Number of marriages in the last year where the couple met online: 17%*

10. *People who dated more than one person simultaneously: 53%*

What do people look for online?

- People who report that common interests are most important: 64%

- People who report that looks are the most important: 49%

What's More Important to Online Daters on a First Date?

- Personality: 30%

- Smile and Looks: 23%

- Sense of Humor: 14%

- Career and Education: 10%

What Do Online Female Daters Prefer?

- Nice Guys: 38%

- Bad Boys: 15%

- Blend of Both: 34%

What Do Online Male Daters Prefer?

- "Modern Career Girl": 42%

- "Girl Next Door": 34%

- "Hottie": 24%

*http://www.statisticbrain.com/online-dating-statistics/

.

2.
WHAT YOU NEED TO KNOW ABOUT ONLINE DATING INCLUDING PROS & CONS

Expect Some White Lies. Although most people don't completely misrepresent themselves, they do have a tendency to embellish in order to put their best (digital) foot forward. For example, someone might say they are 35 instead of 36 to avoid getting filtered out of searches by age on dating sites.

Look at Profiles Like Resumes. This is a postscript to the first thing you need to know. People naturally build their dating profiles so that they can show off their best side, rather than blab about mundane life details. The best way to approach online dating is to browse through profiles as if you were an employer going through a stack of resumes. If someone is a good fit, don't believe they are exactly like they seem to be in their profile. Better to meet in person for an "interview."

Don't Build Someone Up Before You Meet Them. Speaking online can result in intimate communication with someone faster than if you met them in real life. Researchers call this the "hyperpersonal effect." It's common to feel a deep connection with someone you've only chatted with online for a brief period, but don't start imagining your future together too fast. If you've built up an idealized version of a potential mate before you meet them, it can easily spoil a first date in person.

Online Dating Isn't the End All Be All. Yes, it works and is a quick and easy way to meet people, but it will only bring you to the first date. Building a solid relationship with someone, no matter where you meet them, is going to take a lot of work.

Pros of Online Dating

• Access: The world of online dating opens up access to so many more potential partners than you can find in your day to day life. This rings especially true if you are interested in someone with a particular type, lifestyle, orientation, or if you live in an isolated area.

• Matchmaking: Online dating sites offer a variety of personality tests and matching. This can help guide you towards dating potential partners who may be more compatible with you.

• Testing, Testing: Dating online presents you with the opportunity to get to know someone a bit before you meet. This can be a great way to "test" a potential partner if you are a busy person.

• Say Goodbye to Bars: No more bar scenes, unless that is what you really prefer. When you use online dating, you can read about someone, see them in photos and in videos, speak to them on a phone, and make your judgment based on all of this info. With this knowledge, online dating seems superior to meeting someone in a bar because you have a much better idea of what you are getting into.

• Choices Galore: Offline, it is hard to meet people in general, let alone a potential mate. With online dating, you have a range of opportunities and a bunch of choices when it comes down to finding someone you want to date.

• Feel Less Nervous About the First Date: After you get to know someone, chances are you'll have less "first date jitters." You've gotten to know someone well and you've spoken to them on the phone, so it can actually be something to look forward to.

• Cut Down on Guesswork: When you meet someone offline, you have to take time to figure out what they want – what type of relationship they want, if they are open to marriage, kids, or if they are just looking for a hookup. Online dating profiles lay all of this information out for you to get you past this stage. If you are still in doubt before a first date, you can clear things up easily.

• Online Dating Stigma is Over: People aren't living in the stone age anymore – nowadays, most of us have cellphones and the internet. In fact, you're more likely to run into new couples who say "we met online" instead of "we met at a bar."

• The People You Meet Online Actually Want to Date: Although they may want different things than you do, you don't have to feel shy about reaching out to someone. Everyone on a dating site...wants to date.

• Meet People in Your Sweatpants: In the old days, if you wanted to meet people, you had to dress nice, amp yourself up and go out. Nowadays, if you're not in a social mood or you are tired, you can still connect with people online.

• Large Dating Pool: Now that so many people are online dating, there's a ton of options on each network. If you feel you've tapped out your local resources online, take a two or three-week break and let a new group of people roll in.

Cons of Online Dating

• It's crowded in here!: The digital marketplace is crowded and can be exhausting to filter through.

• Matchmakers Aren't Always Right: Matching people perfectly is difficult and personality tests aren't always accurate. Besides, people may be different in person or change. You might wind up on a date with the wrong match, or worse, miss the perfect mate because they didn't perform like you did on your test.

• Computers are Smart but Not That Smart: When you speak to someone online, you are missing out on cues and features that can build the element of attraction, like body language.

• For some people, going online to date can get boring: If you go to a bar to meet people, you're out doing something. This would be a counterpoint to the "meeting people in your sweatpants" online dating benefit.

• Overwhelming: Dating online entails responding to lots of messages, following up, and remembering details about everyone you speak to. It can be overwhelming for a lot of people and takes organization.

• You Might Not Take it to the Limit: When presented with a large pool of potential mates, it might be too tempting to limit your search criteria to more menial things like height, zip code, or income, causing you to miss out on meeting the perfect mate.

• Surprise! Or Not: Knowing what you are getting into decreases anxiety, but some people like the element of surprise and enjoy the excitement of meeting someone new and completely unknown.

• Not Everyone Online is Real: We've all heard stories from friends who went on online dates who met people that didn't look anything like their picture, or straight up lied, rather than embellished facts about themselves.

• It's Easy to Know Someone Too Well Online: If you are speaking to someone who has a complete, honest and detailed profile, you may find that there is no mystery left. When you speak to someone too intimately too quickly, you feel like you already know them. When the first date does happen in real life, you might miss a spark that may have been kindled by the unknown.

• The World Online is a Lot Different Than the World: Speaking to someone through messages is much different than speaking to someone face to face. Sometimes you can get a much better sense of who the person is by speaking to them in the flesh.

• Too Much Info: Having access to all of this knowledge about someone might make you miss out on a good mate. We all make mistakes and wrong turns. A Google search of a name might cause you to shoot someone down that deserves a shot.

• Partner Shopping: The dating pool is so large, that choosing a potential partner can become confusing and overwhelming. If you don't have a clear plan, you might find yourself stuck in a cycle of "partner shopping" - searching for the perfect person, as opposed to actually landing a satisfying relationship.

As you can see, like everything else in life, online dating has its pros and cons. A lot of it comes down to personality and personal preferences. Still not sure if online dating is for you? Or maybe you are ready to take the plunge and aren't sure where to start. Don't worry, we've got you covered! Next, we're going to detail the most popular dating sites so you can have a better idea of where to start. Some sites can be expensive to join, so make sure that you research which one is ideal before signing up for membership.

On one hand, free dating sites are, well, free. On the other hand, online dating sites that charge a fee to join might be likened to a "gated community" of dating. You can be sure that the people on these sites are legitimate, and are serious about meeting someone. Some sites have a mixture of free membership and paid features, as you will see. So let's jump right in and go over the most popular dating sites online!

3.
THE ELEVEN MOST POPULAR DATING SITES (IN NO PARTICULAR ORDER!)

1. Zoosk

Zoosk is an international dating site that you can integrate with Facebook. Serving over eighty countries and available in twenty-five languages, its app is the number one grossing online dating app in the Apple Store.

Zoosk is a good fit for those of you that don't want to get saddled down with questionnaires or building a profile but still want to benefit from a computerized matching algorithm. Zoosk intelligently learns as you click so that it can pair you with potential mates you are likely to be attracted to. So, if you hate taking tests or answering questions on dating sites, this is a definite plus. Zoosk is easy to use, full of people looking for matches and offers a no-frills platform for those of you that hate BS.

Its best feature is that it is approachable for just about anyone, thanks to its direct interface and its large user base. Its main flaw is, that although it offers a guarantee, the monthly pricing is steep for this no-frills dating site. One month will cost you $29.95; the subscription automatically renews unless you cancel. Three months will cost you $59.95, six months will be $79.95.

2. PlentyofFish (POF)

PlentyofFish was one of the first free online dating sites. It has a personality test that measures five factors: self-confidence, self-control, family orientation, "easygoingness," and social dependency/openness. It was started in 2003, and POF generates matches for you with a "statistical model based on thousands of successful couples" who took the chemistry test. Additionally, POF has a mobile app where you can filter based on body type, height or education.

POF is ideal for people that don't want to be charged for a service but want algorithmic matching, and a little buffer time before meeting up with a potential mate offline.

POF has a paid version that features a "Who's Seen Me" button where you can see who has looked at your profile. It can be useful in situations where a member might be a "secret admirer," browsing a profile frequently without communicating. It could be a great way to find people who are interested in you and reach out!

Its best feature is that a large group of members and easy user interface makes using POF as natural as Twitter or Facebook, and the app makes it easy to use the site on the go. Its main flaw is that the site is known for a lot of questionable people that are clearly catfishing/luring people in with a fake persona and profile. POF is free, but you have the ability to pay for added features too.

3. Chemistry.com

Chemistry is a great site for older people looking for matter-of-fact compatibility and a little online dating guidance. Its matching algorithm was crafted by a professor of anthropology and expert on the science of attraction and love. This woman, Dr. Helen Fisher, writes regular blog posts available to members on the site. A neat thing about this site is that it evaluates your activity as you use the site, offering personalized feedback on different aspects of your behavior and profile.

Chemistry offers a straightforward dating platform that is simple to use and full of members.

The best thing about Chemistry is that it is easy to use, so it's a great place to start for people using a dating site for the first time. Its biggest flaw is that it feels a bit dated when you compare it to newer, more modern online dating sites. Chemistry is free to build a profile, but to start messaging, payment is required. For one month, the charge is $49.95. If you sign up for three months, the cost goes down to $33.32 a month, for six months, the price plummets to $26.65.

4. OkCupid

OkCupid caused quite a scene when it was started back in 2004. In the beginning, it was most popular with the 18-35 demographic, but its user base has since expanded beyond this age group. Some sites will only allow you to message users who have been declared a match for you, but OkCupid allows you to message anyone. You can communicate through private messages and instant messages.

OkCupid is ideal for younger people, particularly with its newer app. Younger people who are open to the unconventional, in particular, will enjoy the site best. The site is known for its somewhat quirky matchmaking questionnaire which is always evolving. Questions can be submitted by members, and are reviewed by a select group of users which send them to the OKC staff who then choose the best ones. The site lets you know what percentage of match, enemy, or friend you are with other members. When you fill out each question, you can rate how important the answer is to you, and how important it is that a potential mate answer the same way. For example, perhaps you don't like television but don't mind if your partner is an avid viewer.

OkCupid's best feature is their app and desktop site. Most desktop sites or apps don't make it especially easy to transition from desktop to app, but OKC makes this easy, so you can keep the conversation going. Its biggest flaw is that, although it functions just fine for free, you do have to pay additional fees to be a paid member. (An "A-list" member).

OkCupid is free with the option to pay to be an A-list member. Benefits of doing so include the ability to do advanced searches (like filtering by body type), no advertisements, the option to browse invisibly, and higher placement in search results.

5. LavaLife

LavaLife originally connected people through the telephone – you may remember it if you are old enough! (It started in 1987). However, it has been online since 1997. The site has three sections: intimate encounters, relationships, and dating, and you can have a different profile for each section.

LavaLife is ideal for the older crowd, and people who have an older-school approach to dating – preferring to speak over the phone and computer instead of messaging. The website allows you to communicate in various ways, such as video messaging, phone calls through the site, sharing private photo galleries, and the ability to record a personal profile.

LavaLife offers an easy to use interface and a mainstream, traditional platform to use.

LavaLife's best feature is that it encourages its members to take the conversation offline – whether it's meeting in real life or speaking over the phone, as quickly as possible. Its biggest flaw is that with all of the free dating platforms, it's difficult to justify paying full price to be a member of a dating website with no algorithm or matching features.

You can send "smiles" for free and it's free to reply to a paid member's message. However, to fully participate, you need to pay. It's $34.99 per month if you pay month to month, or $19.99 per month if you pay for three months at once. Six months will cost you $9.99 per month.

6. Match.com

Match is geared for people searching for serious relationships or marriage. You fill out a questionnaire that asks basic lifestyle questions. The questions are straightforward – nothing too quirky, psychological or scientific. The questions let you hone in on a match based on criteria like income, ethnicity, or educational background. Additionally, you can message and call other users from an untraceable number, adding to the security of the site. Match also offers a program called "Stir." Its goal is to bring members together at local events. An app is also available for paid subscribers.

Match is ideal for people looking for a serious relationship. There aren't many catfish or questionable profiles at all, so it's easy to find a similar match.

Match.com's best feature is that it does a great job removing unreliable or untrustworthy profiles. Its biggest flaw is that although paid users can use the app, the desktop site is still dated.

You can send a "smile" to other users, but you do have to pay to begin messaging or calling. One month is $39.99, three months costs $22.99 a month, and for six months, you can choose between a $19.99 a month option or a $20.99 a month option. The $20.99 per month option allows you to have preferential placement in search results, and allows you to see if someone has read your message.

7. eHarmony

eHarmony has a very precise matching algorithm. The questionnaire is about four hundred questions long – the longest of all online dating sites. At the end, there is the possibility you may be rejected from the site if you are not a suitable candidate! The questions are similar to Chemistry's and asks lifestyle questions, like what ethnicity you would like your partner to be, and how much money you earn. You can only message or receive messages by someone who the site has been declared compatible with you.

eHarmony is ideal for professionals or people who are particular about the match they want. They say their site has created 4% of new United States marriages in the last ten years and also has an app.

eHarmony's best feature is its mobile app, making it easy for busy professionals to find matches. Its biggest flaw is ironically the questionnaire you must fill out to join – over 400 questions. Not the best choice for busy professionals.

You can join eHarmony for $59.95 for one month, $39.95 a month for three months, or $29.95 a month for six months. One year is $19.95 a month.

8. HowAboutWe

HowAboutWe is an online dating site that puts importance on the actual date. The site works like this: it asks you the question "How about we..." and you fill in your idea for a first date. This way, you can go offline and meet face-to-face quickly, and the site encourages more interesting dates than just drinks at a bar. The site has been in service since 2010, is available across 30 countries in 15 languages and has over a million users. Basically, instead of filling out a profile, users express themselves through the date they would like to have.

HowAboutWe is ideal for adventurous, creative types that are looking to meet someone right, quick.

HowAboutWe's best feature is its concept: a creative idea and an easy ice breaker. Its biggest drawback is that with the influx of free dating sites and apps, HowAboutWe's price is pretty steep for a site that allows you to answer one question.

You can create a profile, browse through others, and post about dates. But you must pay for membership in order to receive and send unlimited messages, with other things. Memberships start at $8.99 per month and go up to $34.99 per month – depending on what options you would like to choose.

9. Tinder

Tinder has a reputation for being a hookup app as opposed to a dating app, but there are a decent amount of members looking to date in hopes of finding love. This hookup mindset might be in part due to the concept, though – you swipe through pictures of people in your area – if you like what you see, you can "heart" them. If they also push the heart button when they see your picture, you two can message each other. Tinder also links to your Facebook profile, so you can see how many Facebook mutual friends you may have in common with a potential mate.

Although some relationships have been started on Tinder, it is really geared towards casual relationships or hookups than anything serious. It is ideal for bold people who want to meet a lot of new people immediately – no profiles or questionnaires to hold you back.

Tinder's best feature is that you only need to swipe right or left, making it easy and fun to see other users. Tinder's biggest flaw is that it has a host of people looking for hookups only because matches are based on aesthetics.

Tinder is completely free to use.

10. MeetMe.com

MeetMe combines gaming, chatting, and media sharing. The site utilizes gamification to encourage interaction between members with games like "two truths and a lie" and "rate me." Not too long ago, MeetMe launched an app called "Charm" which is kind of a combination of Tinder and Vine. The creators of the app found pictures on dating sites to be inaccurate representations of how people look. Therefore, the app permits you to record and watch short looping videos of other users and yourself. Not only did the app make it more fun, it made it more secure.

MeetMe is ideal for performer types who are not shy and unopposed to making videos.

MeetMe's best feature is its mobile app, Charm, which is more social media-like than other traditional online dating sites. Its biggest flaw is that it is very much targeted to a younger crowd only.

MeetMe is free to join, however, you have the option to upgrade to a premium membership that includes perks such as spotlighting your profile.

11. Spark Network

The Spark Network hones in on finding matches based on cultural, religious and ethnic preferences specifically. It's best known for sites like JDate, Black Singles, and Christian Mingle. Each service is crafted towards presenting members with a private, fun, and easy way of connecting with friends or meeting potential matches. When you register, you fill out a basic survey and are then encouraged to participate in forums, send e-cards, and messages. The Spark Network has nearly a 1 to 1 woman to man ratio. Services such as JDate keeps users up to date with Jewish events, and encourages real life meetings.

Spark Network is ideal for people looking to chat with and meet a match based on demographics, beliefs, and interests.

Its best feature is that the network caters to similar people of the same faith, making it inviting and easy for religious daters to find a match. Its biggest drawback is the dated interface.

Spark Network doesn't charge for basic registration of browsing. For the Black Singles service, six months of using the site is $29.04, for JDate, it is $119.94 for six months, while Christian Mingles is $59.96 for three months.

4.
HOW TO CHOOSE AN ONLINE DATING SITE

If you jump into online dating too quickly, you will find yourself easily overwhelmed and can even procrastinate when it comes to getting started. Have a game plan. Ask yourself how much control you want. Sites like eHarmony suggest potential partners *for* you, while other sites like Match let *you* decide. This is really personal preference. If you have a good idea of the qualities you want in a partner, maybe sites that let you choose who to contact are a better choice for you.

Price is also a factor. While OkCupid and PlentyofFish are free, others can cost up to $60 a month. While free membership is always appealing, the potential matches you might meet could be more interested in a hookup only. Finally, don't ignore smaller sites that embrace your interests. There's less of a "meat market" feel with some of the smaller sites, and you are more likely to find potential matches you can relate to.

Okay, so we went over all of the most popular websites and

why and why not you might be interested in them. As you can see, the type of online dating site that is ideal for you heavily depends on your personality. Once you have chosen which site or sites to use, read these online dating etiquette tips to get a good idea of where to start.

5
ONLINE DATING ETIQUETTE
ADVICE FOR MEN & WOMEN

Advice for Men

Smooth Operator or Super Aggressive?

A lot of men send inappropriate messages to women on dating sites. We'll assume you wouldn't think about doing that! However, it might occur to you that a good tactic is to send a cocky, arrogant or aggressive message, or one mentioning your physical characteristics. Here's a good rule of thumb. If you wouldn't say it to a complete stranger in real life, don't say it online. A better gambit would be actually reading her profile and mentioning something you have in common. If you suspect that you might be sending aggressive messages, write out the message, walk away for ten minutes then return back to the computer. Is this something you would say to a woman on the subway you found attractive? If not, rewrite that message.

Cold feet and Self-Conscious

Don't mention that you aren't sure about online dating, or make some justification as to why you are on the site. Times have changed, and this is considered annoying to more secure women who have no problem using dating sites. It also communicates low confidence because you are pointing out your hesitations. If you have the need to explain yourself, wait until you've met in person, and explain why you joined confidently.

Pick up Line or Immature?

"Are you Jamaican? Cause Jamaican me crazy!" Don't leave messages with silly pickup lines, no matter how clever you think they are. Women realize you are probably using this line on everyone, and too much flattery comes across as insincere. A mature way to flatter a woman might be to remark on her smile.

Don't Live in Denial

If you have been told that the woman you are dating doesn't think you are a good fit, don't take it personally, and let it go. Constantly messaging someone who is clearly not interested in you is a waste of time. The time you could be using to find someone who does think you are good for them.

Don't Delay

If you like a woman and have sent a few messages back and forth, ask her out! It might be frustrating to speak to someone for weeks without being asked out and eventually, your potential match might stop talking to you.

Don't Push it too Quickly

If you are into someone after a few dates, don't do something drastic like demand that she takes her online dating profile down. This is a surefire way to scare a woman away. Allow the woman to let you know when she is ready to date exclusively. Or if you really want to bring it up, phrase it like this: "I'm thinking about taking my profile down. What do you think?"

Don't be Generic

Women are inundated with messages every day. Sending a generic message like "Hi, how are you?" isn't going to make you stand out from the crowd. Try to write something a bit more personal. Mention something you two have in common, like a quote from a movie she listed as one of her favorites.

Online Dating Advice for Women

Keep it Short and Sweet

A dating expert determined that women that showed a little skin (shoulders or cleavage) were most popular on the site. However, she also found that shortening a profile to 100 words is just as effective. Would you want to read through a 1,000-word profile about someone's mundane life details? I'm not saying people live mundane lives, but keep some mystery alive. Don't list every little detail about your life. Keep your profile short and sweet and put the most important things you want your potential match to know in there.

Take Initiative and Suggest a Creative Date

The most common online date is meeting for a quick drink, but this isn't always the best way to get to know someone and what their interests are. Besides, having drinks on a first date can be a potential hazard for women. Suggest a trip to a museum, art gallery or a walk down a scenic bridge instead. It will be great conversation material, and you won't have to worry about who pays/splits the bill.

Don't be Excessively Choosy

When you are online perusing profiles, it's easy to rule someone out because they don't have a great haircut, or don't like the same movies and television shows as you. Does this really matter in the grand scheme of things? Don't focus on looks, focus on how kind the heart of your potential match is and you will be a happy online dater.

Don't Choose a Lengthy Date

Take your time chatting up a potential date, but don't commit to a long date when you meet in real life. You don't want to be stuck in awkward silence for hours if you and your potential match do not click.

Play the Field

Men do it, why can't women? Go on a number of first dates so that you can be sure that the person you pick is the right one for you. When you compare potential matches, you have a better idea of which choice is the best.

Dating Advice for Men and Women

Don't Go Dutch

Taking someone out and being taken out - this smacks of romance. Calculating debt based on who ate the most jalapeno poppers doesn't convey romance at all. A man taking a woman out is a mating ritual that has stood the test of time. This isn't about chivalry – it's about romance. If you are a woman and this idea offends you, more power to you! You should pay the bill then and take your man out for a night on the town – tip and all. It really doesn't matter who pays – the ritual of being taken out and taking one out is important on a first date.

Let Them Go

If you aren't feeling it with someone you thought you liked, do the right thing. Don't just stop returning calls. You wouldn't like wondering why somebody you liked isn't returning your calls. You don't have to be specific, if you aren't feeling someone, let them know over the phone (not via text) that you just don't think you are compatible. Chances are the other party will respect your opinion. That's what's great about the world of online dating. Sure, you might strike out, but you can always go back online and find someone more compatible for you.

Zip it, Lock it, Keep it in Your Pocket

Try to listen to the other party on the date effectively. We understand you might be nervous and as a result may yammer on about yourself. But, if you have a tendency to do this, now might be a good time to improve your listening skills. The best way to listen more effectively on a first date is to practice. Jot down a list of questions. Don't whip out the list during the date – that might be weird. But memorize some of the questions and be sure to ask your date all about themselves. People like to talk about themselves, so if you want a successful first date, sit back, relax, and let your date do so. Every so often, when they say something, rephrase what they said and say it back to them to indicate that you are empathetic and actively listening.

Example: So you're saying you'd like to make a career change sometime in the future?

Be Proud of Who You Are, Despite the Fact That This Will Get You Rejected

Be authentic. If you are a quirky person, don't hold back. If you don't agree with a date's opinion on politics, if this matters to you, speak up, but calmly. This person doesn't know you yet, and you don't want to scare them away. Yes, if you meet up with the wrong person you might get rejected. It is easy to see that the more you express who you really are, the greater the risk that you will be rejected. Have the confidence to be yourself, to disagree if you do (again calmly and politely), and you will save yourself wasted time with incompatible matches and put yourself on the fast track to the perfect mate when you do meet someone that clicks. Remember, in the world of online dating to not take rejection personally.

Don't be Shallow Online! You Aren't Shallow in Real Life, Are You?

Behind the anonymity of being online, it is easy to have unrealistically high expectations, and to be a bit, well, shallow. Especially with apps like Tinder, where you judge users solely on their looks. Every time you turn someone down because they aren't as attractive as you think they should be, you are missing the opportunity to possibly connect to someone perfect for you. It's important to have priorities and standards when you date, but these standards should measure a person's behavior, not their appearance.

Don't Hone in on the Little Things

He likes the Simpsons and you love Friends. Is this really a deal breaker? Does it matter what bars, books, or movies a person likes when it comes to love? Here are some things you should mull over: Is she a kind person? Does he seem intelligent? Does she have integrity? What are her priorities? If you think you are above someone because they have a job you consider menial, think again. Too often, in the United States, we measure success with the wrong yardstick.

Focus on the Profile Tone

Writers speak about tone in their copy, content, essays and books. "The definition of tone is the way the author expresses his attitude through his writing." http://examples.yourdictionary.com/examples-of-tone-in-a-story.html Tone is what is important when you look at online dating profiles. What you need to do is read between the lines. Look for signs of boastfulness, bitterness or a snide attitude. Keep an eye out for insincerity.

For example, there's that person who "absolutely loves" his life just the way it is. He is completely satisfied with everything in his life. He joined the site on a lark – his friend suggested it and he said to himself, "why not?" These are red flags because nobody is completely satisfied with their life. People don't join dating sites on a whim, sincere people join dating sites to find a mate to complete them. So read between the lines. If someone is so happy with their life, they may have trouble being honest about their vulnerability, or even worse, don't have virtuous motives.

Read between the lines and look for a well-adjusted mate.

Someone who is pleasant, reasonable and friendly. Someone who would be your best friend even if you hate his taste in music or don't share the same movie preferences.

Don't take People's Own Claims About Themselves at Face Value

Across dating websites, you will see assertions like "I'm an incurable optimist," or, "I have a great sense of humor about myself. Nothing can offend me." *Read between the lines* because people tend to exaggerate, but more importantly, the way we see ourselves often is not the way others see us. Read between the lines, but pay attention to what rises to the surface – like a sense of humor through the writer's tone. This says more about what she is like in person than reading a profile that says "I am a funny person." The only claims you should take at face value are facts – what is their job, their education level, where are they located? And you should even keep an open mind about that.

Don't Make Snap Judgments Based on a Profile

Let's face it. Online dating is a great way to meet people, but you just won't know if he is the ideal match for you until you meet him in real life. Maybe you fell in love with the fact that he claims to love animals, but you don't know his manner and demeanor. What if he is horribly rude to your waitress? How about eye contact, tone of voice, or if your date even smiles? You also have to wait to meet someone in person to find out if they are polite. Will they make an effort to ask you questions? Will he be checking out other women while you sit across from him, or will she be constantly checking her phone?

Never be Afraid to be Alone

It's easy to get tired of dating and want to rush into a relationship. However, getting attached too soon can kill a connection, or scare off a potential mate. We know you want to find "the one" but that is a tall order – to do that you need to take time and patience, online or offline.

So now you've been introduced to the etiquette of online dating. At least, we've presented some food for thought. But what's next? Read the next section on how to effectively approach online dating.

6
HOW TO EFFECTIVELY APPROACH
ONLINE DATING

Before you even sign on to a dating website, develop a strategy, just like everything else in life. Do you know what you are looking for? Make a mental list and be specific with what matters.

You should choose a list of the most important personality traits you desire, and things that are really important. For example, could you date a single mother? Does your mate need to want kids? Prioritize like this: instead of demanding that a partner sit on your side of the political spectrum, demand that they share the same values as you and have the same moral compass.

Prioritize!

Once you have come up with all of the traits you desire in a mate, put them in priority order. To help you do this, think about your previous relationships. What did you like? What did you hate? Think about your favorite friends and family members. What draws you to them? Go ahead and make your *own* dating algorithm.

Keep Your Profile Short

Think like a marketer writing a commercial. Keep your profile short and intriguing. Communicate the most important things about you. Jump into the shoes of an advertiser when you write your profile.

Save Sarcasm for the Date

Sarcasm may cause you to think you sound clever, but unfortunately, in print, without facial expressions or inflection in the tone of your voice, you may come across as mean or angry. Here's a rule of thumb if you integrate sarcasm into your sense of humor heavily: after you have written your profile, have someone else read it to you. How does it sound?

Don't be Phony, but be Optimistic

Write about what excites you, or craft a picture of a really fantastic day you would love to be a part of.

Think Like a Marketer

Marketers understand that "the medium is the message." That means they paint different pictures for Twitter, Facebook, and Youtube. If you are on multiple dating sites, think like a marketer. Understand who your audience is, what you want, and what "call to action" you can use to hook the people who matter to you.

Be Honest

Your profile can be both compelling and honest. Honesty

communicates the fact that you are comfortable in your own skin, and that you have integrity. Everyone is looking for these qualities.

Don't Cross the Line

Don't post photos that are overly sexy, whether you are male or female. Keep your profile appropriate and disclose life details as you get to know someone, much like you would if you had met someone in real life.

Be Kind to Yourself If You Are Rejected

Compassion, compassion, compassion. There are a million and one reasons why someone might reject you that has absolutely nothing to do with *you*. Do not take it personal. Trust that if you are being rejected, it's because there is someone better suited for you.

So now you know some things about the online world of dating. However, just like in the real world, not everyone is looking out for your best interest. There are people on dating sites called "catfish" - online criminals who aren't who they say they are. In fact, someone you are talking to, that you think is one town over, may not even be from the same country! Here are some ways to protect yourself from these unsavory individuals.

7
THROWING BACK CATFISH – HOW TO AVOID ONLINE SCAMS

Unfortunately, some people have moral compasses that don't measure up to yours. They may rationalize hurting others to secure their own financial stability.

These people are criminals. And these criminals are not afraid to target the most vulnerable targets – women over forty, divorcees, widows, disabled people - however, every demographic and age group is at risk.

Fortunately, these people are not very innovative. Most catfish scams are extremely similar: the victim is contacted by a catfish who appears interested. The discussion is usually lengthy – weeks, even months of chatting back and forth while the catfish ferrets out your vulnerabilities and builds false confidence.

The catfish has no problem escalating the romance and professing their love. But something always holds them back from actually meeting you. When the catfish is certain that they have you in their clutches, they will request money. They are not above emotional extortion or manipulation. One woman on one scamming site reported that a catfish told her that his daughter was in the hospital and needed care.

Over and over, the catfish seems to have incredibly bad luck, facing hardship after hardship that only you can help them with by giving them money. Another thing the catfish might do is ask you to send money overseas, or receive an item like a laptop and mail it somewhere else.

What is really going on? You have been targeted by a criminal, or more likely, a group of criminals who lifted pictures from other websites and crafted fake profiles to match your interests. Now you have lost money to someone who is trying to manipulate and hurt you, or even worse, you may have taken part in criminal activity yourself. (Remember that laptop? It was stolen. The checks you cashed were stolen. The money you sent overseas was laundered.) These are professional criminals you are dealing with. They know what they are doing and they know what works, therefore, it is important to be aware of them and the way they work.

Another, more vicious scheme, is when a catfish meets victims online and asks them to move the conversation to another social networking site. Talk then turns intimate. Later, victims are sent a link to a website – the conversations are posted there, their photos are there, as well as their phone numbers. To remove the information, you must make a payment. But at this point, with this degradation of integrity, there is no way to believe this bargain will be upheld.

Being taken in by a catfish can be mortifying – particularly if you have intimate photos or conversations posted online.

But it is important to file a complaint with the FBI Internet Crime Complaint Center. Www.ic3.gov When you do this, you are making the online dating community safer for everyone.

Catfishing can be pretty scary stuff! Don't stress out too much. Fortunately, a lot of catfish use the same MO and there are attributes, personality traits, and other identifying information can help you to filter out catfish from your list of suitors.

Recognizing an Online Dating Scam Artist

Look for these red flags:

-Your romantic interest wants you to leave the dating site and communicate through email, text or instant messages

-Your romantic interest immediately declares feelings of love

-Your romantic interest emails a photograph that looks like it came from "Glamour magazine" or, on the other hand, is of very bad quality.

-Your romantic interest says they are from the US but they are traveling or working overseas

-Your romantic interest is constantly making plans to visit you but is prevented from doing so because of a tragic event

-Your romantic interest asks for money

-Your romantic interest wants to send you items like a laptop or cellphone elsewhere. Worse, they may ask you to accept money into your bank account, and ask you to transfer it to someone else.

One way to steer clear of these criminals altogether is to stick to online dating websites with nationally known reputations. Finally, the FBI advises not to send money through any wire transfer service to someone you met online. The chances of recovering your money are very slim. If you believe you are the victim of an online dating scam or any Internet-facilitated crime, please file a report at www.ic3.gov.

https://www.fbi.gov/contact-us/field-offices/sandiego/news/press-releases/fbi-warns-of-online-dating-scams

These are some telltale signs of catfish, but there is still more you should know. The more you know about online dating schemes, the more you can protect yourself and the dating community in general. Read on to find out what else you should know about catfishes and catfish schemes online.

What Else You Should Know About Catfish

-Catfish can do more than just embarrass you and scam you out of money. They may pose a risk to your personal safety. Many catfish are members of international crime networks. You may even be lured overseas, which can put you in danger with a tragic outcome.

-Catfish want you to leave the dating site because online dating sites will remove members who are problematic. This gets in their way of scamming the next victim. The most common excuse is "My membership is almost up. Can we communicate through text or email?"

-You need to be realistic. If you are a 58-year-old man, why is a twenty-six-year-old woman who looks like a model suddenly telling you that she loves you? Or vice versa, if you are a 58-year-old woman, why is a twenty-six-year-old man suddenly telling you that he loves you?

-You should be on guard if you are what scammers consider vulnerable – in the age bracket of 50 or 60, divorced, widowed, or if you have a weight problem or are recovering from an illness.

-Watch out for excessive indications of wealth. Yes, real people sometimes have nice cars and vacation in expensive resorts, but online scammers typically will show you pictures of expensive cars, mansions, and exotic backgrounds to convince you they are wealthy, so any money they ask for is a loan.

-Head to Google images to match a suspicious suitor to a real person. You can search by image and see if a catfish has lifted a picture of a model, or a man with expensive items.

-Pay attention to indications that someone who says they are from the U.S. is really a foreigner. Look for strange sentence structures, word choices and bad grammar. If you notice these anomalies, ask your romantic interest many questions. Where are they from? Where were they educated? Again, be realistic. If your match is from Harvard but can't pump out a coherent sentence, this is cause for suspicion.

Look for these Suspicious Signs:

- Self Employed professional working overseas

- A widower with a child

- Someone who says they live near you, are currently away but will be returning soon.

Look for discrepancies:

- Your match says they have been away but their profile shows that they are online

- Their profile references areas that are not close to where they live

- Pronouns may be mixed up – for example using him instead of he

- Things they mention that are unrelated to their profile.

- Someone giving you information that seems too revealing, or unbelievable

If you are interested in someone who strikes you as suspicious, insist on a phone call. Does this person have a slight accent? Do they understand slang? Ask them probing questions – it is far easier to lie online when you have the time to as opposed to in real time on the phone.

Examine the phone number area code. If the area code doesn't match the area in which they say they live, this is typically an indication that they don't live in the country at all.

Finally, look for the catch. Financial emergencies will suddenly appear. If you don't send the money, the catfish will likely question your trust, saying if there is no trust, there is no relationship. Don't buy it.

Do not become emotionally attached before you take all of these precautions. We all know how emotions can blind us from seeing the truth. You want to do your homework before you start to develop feelings for someone. There is nothing worse, I'm told, than falling in love with a fake person who is only out for financial gain. These criminals are patient and know how to work their way into a vulnerable person's life, so if you look for these signs at the start, you will be well prepared and save yourself a lot of time and energy.

There's another danger lurking in the world of online dating that, with the right precautions, you can avoid. This danger is suitors (male or female) with not so virtuous motives. It is important to put your physical safety first when you go to meet someone for the first time. At best, you can avoid an awkward premature make out session in someone's car. At worst you can save your life.

How to be Safe When You Are Online Dating

Percent of sex offenders who use online dating to meet people -10 %

Unfortunately, not everyone deserves the benefit of the doubt, as you have read above. Although online dating, for the most part, is safe, you may find yourself in danger if you aren't cautious - especially if you are a woman. Follow these tips to protect yourself:

-Preserve your identity: Cyber stalking is also very real. Don't use your real name on your profile, post your phone number, address, or anything else that may put you in harm's way if any of that information fell into the wrong hands.

-Choose a well-known dating service: Choose a dating site with a long-term reputation. Look for features like anonymous technology or phone services where you can call other users without divulging your phone number.

-Play detective. Ask lots of questions and notice the way a person writes. Beware of people who are too pushy or eager. Beware of irritability, excessive bragging, or anger. Ask about past relationships.

-If you are really worried, but still interested, be open about this. If the other person has nothing to hide, it will not bother them. You can even ask your romantic interest to snap a selfie holding today's newspaper. You may feel silly asking, but this request could save you from a world of hurt.

-With everyone you speak to, whether you are suspicious of them or not, keep copies of all correspondence. If you have problems in the future, be it online, or if you become a victim of cyberstalking, physical proof is essential.

-Don't be afraid to block and/or report anyone who is making you feel uncomfortable or who is harassing you.

-Google your romantic interest's profile handle in quotes and without. For example, if someone's profile name is "happy go lucky", Google it just like that, within the quotes. Many people are on multiple sites, using the same profile name. This in itself isn't cause for worry. But what you might do is ask this person if they are on only one dating site and see what they say.

-Listen to your gut. If something seems fishy, it probably is. If something feels off, trust it.

-Realize that there's a lot of information about you online. Your office location is on LinkedIn. Your address is tagged on your Instagram posts. Your phone number may be linked to a Craigslist ad where you were trying to sell an old bookshelf. That being said, don't provide your last name, address, or any other identifying information online.

If you are hurt or have been victimized by a catfish, don't despair. There are measures you can take to bring this person to justice, or at least make sure nothing similar happens to anyone else in the world of online dating.

What Do I Do if I Have Been Catfished or Hurt?

Now is the time to be brave. If you don't report what happened, the wrongdoer will repeat his or her actions or even escalate them. Do NOT blame yourself. If you have been assaulted in any way, remember that even if you did not say no, you did not say yes either. Immediately report any type of offense to a dating site. If you have been involved in a scam, contact the FBI's Internet Crime Complaint Center and the Attorney General of your state.

There are many ways you can protect yourself when you

first meet someone online. Take these recommendations for as many dates as you need to feel completely comfortable being around someone alone:

How to Protect Yourself When You Meet an Online Date

1. Trust Your Gut. If something about the person you have just met is making you uncomfortable, something is wrong. If a situation feels shady, it probably is. You are never obligated to continue an online interaction or even a date.

2. Meet in a public place that is well lit – arrive on your own and leave on your own. Do NOT let your date pick you up or drop you home. Let someone else close to you know about your plans to go on an online date, and avoid excessive consumption of alcoholic beverages on a first online date. A better idea is abstaining completely.

3. Don't be afraid to ask a close friend to give you a call mid-date that you can answer if you feel uncomfortable. Always let someone know who you are meeting, where, when and for how long. If you are feeling cautious, you may ask a friend to hang out at the place where you meet to keep a discrete eye on you from across the room.

4. Never respond to a person's request for nude pictures. You can show your face in a selfie, but be sure you're wearing clothes in the picture! It is far too easy to post intimate photos online for everyone to see. Remember, nothing online is private. Once it's out there, it's out there for good.

5. If you have been victimized in any way, you should

report the abuse. You may contact the local authorities, as well as websites to help others who have been victimized online, like www.haltabuse.org and www.romancescams.org. When you do this you are protecting yourself and others.

6. Choose a larger, more reputable site, or a smaller niche site that requires payment to join. Larger sites like OkCupid, eHarmony, and Match.com can typically also be trusted to protect your private information.

7. Make sure you verify your online match is who they say they are by searching where else their pictures might be posted. For example, their dating profile picture might be the same as their Facebook profile picture. People tend to filter themselves less on social media sites, so this is a way to find out if they have some distasteful personality traits. You can also copy the profile picture of someone you are planning on meeting into Google Image search to determine if your match is using a fake photo of an old celebrity or a model.

Using a secure dating site can make all of the difference when it comes to protecting yourself and your person when you do take the dive and go for the first date. Here are some questions you should ask to locate the safest dating sites for you to use.

Questions You Should Ask Yourself to Find Secure Dating Sites

- Does the online dating site screen candidates?

- What steps does the website take to lower the level of abuse?

- If abuse occurs, how does the site handle it?

- Does the site allow explicit content in its terms of service?

- Does the online dating site take the time to review videos, chats, and webcams?

- Are there tips provided that informs users how to safely navigate the site in order to avoid predators?

- Does the site list an emergency phone number?

- Does the online dating site run users through a registered sex offender database?

8.
IF MARRIAGE IS THE MOTIVE

---

*"Love is like a virus. It can happen to
anybody at any time. ~ "Maya Angelou*

We make one critical assumption of a person's motive when engaging in online dating. Be warned that the numbers that make up the body of statistics for this industry includes individuals who have no intention of tying the knot. Nonetheless, we make this assumption to facilitate our central thesis that online dating might not be the best place to find your future mate for a large segment of the singles population.

Getting married to a person is not about love. I know this is a very hard concept to grab. But after much research, study, and evaluations, it rings true. A position in opposition of this is purely a romantic's view. It is, of course, unrealistic to say that the euphoric feeling many young couples feel as love doesn't exist. It does exist indeed. First falling in love and the high it can product is addicting. The euphoria is nature's reward system to bring both sexes together with the final objective of preserving the species into the next generation. That euphoria is to love as cocaine is to happiness. Some say that being addicted to love is much like an addiction to cocaine. Neither addiction is healthy, and true happiness is not the result of one or the other. If you need one or the other to be happy, you will be sadly disappointed. You see many people, nowadays, getting married 2 or 3 or even 4 times. Many of these people have been searching for happiness outside of themselves. When the euphoric feeling of love dissipates (as it will), they begin to search for it elsewhere, in another mate, where the cycle will continue.

True love is not a feeling. Can your tongue feel itself? Can your teeth feel themselves? Can your ear hear itself? No. When something becomes a part of you, you don't feel it anymore. More on this later.

We must also be pragmatic about the fact that nature does not need a wedding license to orchestrate the next generation. Weddings, marriages, vows and even monogamy are not needed to produce the next generation. For that matter, either is dating. All these concepts, have no basis in nature, yet have been proven to be best practices, over time. Some naturalists propose that not everything that nature comes up with is the right solution. Sometimes the path humans take is impacted by the ability of the human mind to peer into the future. We use logic, reasoning and we learn from suboptimal outcomes of the past to develop ways and means to a better outcome in the future.

Those who believe that nature hasn't always come up with the right solution, believing that maybe nature does make mistakes, believe that those mistakes are not the hallmark of ignorance or foolish design. Mistakes are the root of learning and improving. Take for instance the fact that initial life of the insect and animal kingdom was asexual. It turned out that for the conditions that were present at the time and most of the conditions now, the asexual nature of gene distribution and species cultivation was not the best it could be. In asexual reproduction, there is almost zero difference in genetic profile from parent to child. This poses severe problems which some might call a mistake. Then there was a mutation and the single sex, split in two. Judging from that single-sex perspective, it may have seemed like such an aberration.

Without going through an entire lecture on how things have changed and evolved, suffice to say that life on earth went through that split and the two genders evolved pretty much in lockstep. But the key to understanding this whole thing is to realize that the historical and evolutionary forces that predate our consciousness was not running at its optimal level with single species reproduction.

The idea to split the gender emerged from a mutation. That mutation created a change, which divided the character profile between what we now know as masculine and feminine. Fast forward to present times and what we have are two versions of the same species. We call them gender, but think about that for a second, we have two human beings that don't look alike at all. Because, aside from survival biology, our purpose biology, although adaptive, is rather different. Those differences make us distinct. But what it also does is make us like two pieces of a two-piece jigsaw puzzle - both shaped differently, both having a different fragment of an image in the face, but on its own are incomplete. However, when you put those two pieces together, you get the whole picture.

That analogy of the puzzle is crisp, it's unproblematic and it's essentially true. Except for one thing, human beings are anything but static. We change over time, unlike the two pieces of the puzzle. That shift is seismic and causes rifts and stresses between the genes causing each gender to take solace in their fraternal comrades.

Even though taking the easy road is tempting, overcoming it is the hard work that makes for a better marriage.

How is this related to online dating?

In the separation of profiles, the subconscious is a fabulous judge of character. When two people meet, the attraction that results, aside from physical attraction, is based on how our subconscious sees the other person and understands how that person's puzzle piece fits with our own puzzle piece. Online dating obviates that and renders the power and benefit of our subconscious moot when we do not meet in person.

9.
THE ROOTS OF LOVE

Lasting love is not a feeling; it is a decision. It is exclusive before it becomes mutual. As paradoxical as that may seem, the truth in that is profound and forms the central pillar of a loving relationship between a couple.

Love is exclusive because it does not depend on whether the other person loves you back. You love the person for who they are, not for what they give you. This is simple logic. How we love, and how much we love are qualitative and quantitative questions that are misunderstood and misapplied.

When you truly love someone, you take that person in. Do you have feelings for your knee? No. Do you protect it? No, you protect yourself by not allowing harm to come to your knee, however. It's the same with a person you love. They are no longer external to you, they are you.

That youness is what love is and it is exclusive and unconditional.

Does that sound like something you can build when you hookup online? Well, the answer to that is vague at best. Because it doesn't really matter where you meet a person, what matters is what you decide and what your subconscious says about that person. So, there really is no relationship between where you meet a person and whether you can choose to nurture true love.

But here is where the problem arises, and we will look at this deeper in later chapters. When you place a string of people on a carousel and you get to slide through them based on looks and pedestrian qualities, you are completely short-circuiting the process that ordinarily exists. What you are essentially doing is trading in qualitative processes where you get to use your selective instinct and giving that up for quantitative benefits of large quantities and possible benefits from the law of averages to find the right person for you.

The opposite of that is that you may actually find someone, but you may also miss the right one because you ended up wasting time with the wrong one. Choice is not always what it's cracked up to be. You have the freedom to choose but that doesn't mean that you need to sample everything at the buffet table. While you have the freedom of actually doing it, it may give you a tummy ache.

The roots of love can be harder to grow if you expose yourself to the online dating scene. When you have so many to choose from and all you have are superficial characteristics to rely on, you can lose focus on what is important.

As you slide through profiles and pictures on dating sites, remember someone else is doing the same to you. Aren't you more than some of your aesthetic features? Aren't you more than what you can possibly pen in a brief description. Aren't you more than what an algorithm can classify you as? Yes, you are. And so is the person you just scanned over. That doesn't make you superficial. It makes you human.

But being human is exactly what you need in order to find a person to love in real life and not in some online meeting place where you are not able to see the real person and you cannot present your real case.

Real love is about making a decision to be with the person that your subconscious says you are a good match with. You need to trust your subconscious and learn to trust that which is the voice of your subconscious.

The roots of love grow in exclusion, but combine to feed and nourish the tree of life. When you surrender to love (not to the person) you end up loving the person unconditionally. But that potential unconditional love needs focus and a daily renewal of a decision to stay in love (not stay in a state of euphoria). That is what a marriage certificate simulates when it is in place.

The bond of love is sometimes not strong enough to withstand the flailing arms of frustration when the two opposing characters confront the other. The rage momentarily overwhelms the love, and if wasn't for marriage, it would make it highly likely that the couple would walk away from each other. That is the use of the marriage certificate and the vows that accompany it during the festivities.

However, marriage in itself is not love. Marriage is like the rope that ties the carpenter ties around two pieces of wood that he has just set with glue. While the bonds of the glue form and hold the two pieces together, it is the rope that keeps them from falling apart. That is the purpose of marriage - it gives time for love to take root.

What does this have to do with online dating?

Online dating can objectify both genders to the other. It puts the viewer into a frame of mind similar to that of picking out a dress or picking out a garage tool. It objectifies in a way that can have a lasting impact.

Think about what it says when you stand in judgment of another human being and consciously accept or reject based on features and profiles. But let's take that one step further.

There are algorithms these days that help one customer hook up with another customer based on things that they have most in common with each other.

10.
AUCTION SITES AND MEAT MARKETS

When you go on to an auction site you look at a potential purchase as a choice. And that is perfectly fine as you have the freedom to choose whatever you want. Especially when what you are buying is an inanimate object that will run the course of its usefulness in a time scale measured by weeks or months, and then get discarded. Most of the time the trashing of it comes with little or no second thought. That's because these are mere articles of use. They are objects that you come across and you move on after using them. Some people use dating sites in the same way.

The human mind has a built-in statistics and probability analyzer. It is the same place that gives rise to some of our biases and it is the same place that makes us take note of patterns in things around us. Subconsciously we understand patterns and statistics of things happening around us.

Researchers have conducted these experiments on kids and what they found gives us an amazing insight into how we see and process things that we know and don't know. The part of that research that is relevant to the topic at hand has to do with our inherent ability to record statistical information. When we see something happen, more often than not, we instinctively give the occurrence of that, even in the next instance, a higher chance of happening.

But this ability is abused unconsciously by most people. Because perception is unique to each person and his or her background, that element of perception skews the statistical ability of each person. However, what is does do is that it instinctively records each event and draws a correlation to it in other areas.

When applying that to the dating scene, what we find is that most dates don't go anywhere for one reason or the other. There is the compatibility issue and the fact that the person's subconscious is not involved in the selection process. This just makes the chance of success worse off. When this happens over time, and the selection process keeps yielding suboptimal partners, the law of averages start to speak against a possible union.

It starts to feel like it's just not meant to be. That feeling is mixed in with self-doubt and the possibility that there is no one out there who is compatible. What becomes worse is that instead of showcasing the strength of difference between the genders, Dating sites tend not to emphasize the benefit of differences in relationships, and further, the difficulty in finding a match from online dating sites seems to foster the notion that there are more differences that might sometimes be irreconcilable and not just differences that come and go and may strengthen a relationship.

As the potential dates role from one person to the next, faith in the process and in oneself dwindles and expectations against hope increase. After a point, the person is willing to compromise and settle with the first partially acceptable suitor.

None of this level of rejection happens in the real world of dating and social interaction. One of the main reasons for this is that when you meet a person, the chances are you are not looking for anything, and the subconscious mind in you is given a front seat view of the person. If there is a match in its calculation, then you take it from there and more often than not, your subconscious gets it right.

Compared to dating sites, meeting at the local pub or library, which themselves are such clichés, is a better option. The downside that it all boils down to is that your intuition is not given the chance to help you in your shortlisting of candidates. You can't always just rely on the profile picture. Assuming it's even the right picture, a 2D representation of a 4-dimensional person is grossly inadequate in many cases, and completely misleading in most. A lot of people are known to use pictures that represent them in the best way possible, and not as they really appear in everyday life. Some even use photo enhancing programs to hide blemishes, scars, and wrinkles.

The other downside of dating online is that you place yourself at physical and emotional risk. Getting out in your area, becoming more involved in social events, volunteering, and joining something local puts you in better position than any online dating site could ever hope to match up to.

Indeed, the younger and upcoming generation that has held a computer in the palm of their hand from the time before they could walk, can't be ridiculed if they want to think that relationships can be sparked and created through their mobile devices. From the time they get their first smartphone to the time they get their first job, social media, is an extension of who they are and so online dating sites, which are a form of social media in their own right, become part of their ecosystem.

There doesn't seem to be any indication that this trend will wane in the near future. As such it is best that best practices be understood and that online dating be kept social and not made into being the foundational institution of family.

11.
IS THERE A DOWNSIDE TO DATING ONLINE?

Effectively, although it is not positioned so, online dating is not so much about dating to find a soul mate, as it is about socializing to have a good time. There are two broad camps of people that go onto these sites. First there is the group that is looking for something to take flight so that they may have a future - these are the purists, as it were. They take dating sites as dating sites and have every intention of meeting someone with whom they can possibly share a future.

The second group is made up of people who are just there to have a good time. They are not genuine about taking it to a more serious level. At worst, they are there as predators; at best, they cannot be relied on to take the dating to the next non-physical level.

The first camp is in the minority. They are the ones that are ever the optimist. The second camp is well populated by both, men and women.

The problem arises because the true intentions of the person you pick, or the person who picks you, is never fully known with any degree of certainty. The misalignment of expectations, the ulterior intention of participants, the over expectations of how things should unfold, and the possibility of mischief all point toward a risky endeavor at best, and heartbreak at worse.

But the biggest downside is that online dating severs your ability to participate in real relationships. The one thing that most people avail themselves of in an online relationship is the freedom to create a new persona when given the opportunity to stand behind a screen and an avatar. Of course, in most cases, the truth eventually gets flushed out, but that just drives the first point out - that it teaches participants who go through a few of these that online dating can be more trouble than it's worth.

When you meet and date in real life, without the cyber intermediary, you step forward on real footing. You meet people with almost no expectation because you are just going through life. You are not going through a dating site because you are there to read poetry. So the fact that you are admittedly there for finding a date ironically throws a wrench into your psychology.

The physical danger of online dating is quite obvious. It comes back to not really knowing who the other person is even in the wake of one's best efforts at looking at profiles and searching for information. When you know someone in real life, there is a structure behind that person that gives validity to that person and it gives you assurance that the person is legit and the person is harmless. Online, cold introductions do not have the same sort of assurances.

Between women and men, the ones that seem to face the

possibility of danger more often are the women. There have now been a number of horror stories reported in the medium of predators who have gone on to seduce and rape women that they have gone out on dates with after meeting them on online dating sites. The old adage of if it's too good to be true, it probably is, comes to mind because some of the profiles that these predators assume and personify are ones that are too good to be true.

The danger is indeed real because it doesn't stop at online intimidation, but can go on to inflict physical harm. Fatality is not out of the question, unfortunately, and most hate to even talk about it, but it does happen, therefore, becoming aware of it is the key to helping to prevent it. It is always smart to take safety measures when getting involved with online dating.

There is another danger and which is not physical but dangerous nonetheless and these are the identity thieves who stock on vulnerable men and women. Sometimes the person posing to be a really sweet and good looking girl may just be a cyber thief preying on victims to steal their identity and go on to access online bank accounts or other valuables.

Here are some of the tell-tale signs that you should be aware of if you do decide to dip your toes into the online dating pool.

First off, be very weary of someone who is trying to move too quickly. There is not a predetermined or prescribed rate that anything should move at, but you will know it when you get into the situation when someone is pushing to take it to the next level. Slow it down, or get off the track. Moving too fast is a classic tell-tale sign of a potential scam operation ahead.

The next is to make sure the person never asks for money. Anyone who starts to cry over financial difficulties within a short dating window is not someone you can trust. Logic dictates that if a person is in trouble, it didn't happen overnight, and if it didn't happen overnight, how is it they have been in the mood to get onto an online dating site. Ask yourself this, if you have an ongoing financial problem would you be spending time on an online dating site? Most people wouldn't.

The third major tell-tale sign is when there are inconsistencies in basic facts over the period of a few conversations. If you do enter the online dating scene, make sure that you get in a few good long chats and take note of what he or she says. Keep track of it so that you don't get duped by someone who is a predator. When a person changes basic facts, it's a sure sign that they are lying.

Finally, a normal person keeps normal hours. If this person travels a lot or is only available sporadically and then not available at any other time; or if there is a person that has a problem sharing contact information after a certain time, then those are scary signs that most of what this person has to offer is not on the up and up.

There are plenty of dangers out there, and when you get behind a keyboard the problems don't go away, they just take on a higher level of sophistication.

12.
DATING AND MARRIAGE

---

*"5% of Americans who are in a marriage
or committed relationship say they met
their significant other online."* ~
Pew Research

When you compare the statistic above with the fact that more than 50 million adults try dating online, you start to see the efficacy of online dating, especially if your intention is to find a person you want to marry.

Online dating is better suited to social interactions and you may actually increase your chances of meeting the right person there if you walk into the interaction with that mind frame. Because that way, there are no expectations.

Having set the foundation to make the case against online dating specifically for the purpose of finding a marriage partner, let's just now agree that online dating is a great way to meet new friends. Group dates are fun too, and you can mitigate some predatory concerns if you follow a few rules and general guidelines.

For instance, if you meet someone online, you should conduct video calls before you actually meet that person in real life. There are so many video call options today, and most of them are free. Many online dating portals offer this free of charge as well. There is no excuse for someone to decline unless of course they have something to hide, or they are extremely shy about their appearance. Neither is a flattering prospect. Insist early in the introduction that video calls might be a good way to get to know one another.

But it doesn't end there, just because you have a few video calls doesn't mitigate the risk down to zero. You must then focus your attention on the content of the conversation. You have to know what the person is about. Do know that a lot of these predators are skilled hucksters. The women know exactly what to say or how to behave to get the unsuspecting man to do what they want him to do, and there are very suave men who know how to prey on trusting women. These people are trained to trick and scam people.

Once you have observed them visually and evaluated the content of the conversation, you should do a sanity check and get a feel for what they say. Remember, though, not every one of them is a con artist. But you do have to look out for those who are already married and are using dating sites as an easy way to have affairs. So, keep a lookout for suspicious behavior and odd conversation moments. Trust your instincts.

The typical lies that people tell in online dating scenarios can at times seem to depend on gender. Men tend to lie about their income, marital status, and education. Women, on the other hand, have been reported to lie about age, weight, and physical build.

Be careful of expectations for sex on the first date. One of the reasons that online dating sites are so popular and why guys spend a ton of money here is that they are certain that one in three girls will sleep with them on the first date. Now this is not intended to judge or pass commentary on whether sleeping with someone you just met on the first date is appropriate. However, it is without a doubt, dangerous. In addition to that, most guys know this, and so you can expect that the expectation for sex on the first date is fairly high. Don't feel pressured to be the 1 in 3. Be strong, and respect yourself.

I have a male friend, who has been a member of several online dating sites for several years. He is looking for a long-term relationship. He is a great guy and has many great qualities. But I have known him almost all my life. He has always said that if a woman sleeps with him on the first date, he will not contact her again. He feels that if she will sleep with him on the first date, she will sleep with all others on the first date, too, and he can't respect that. He has had many first dates, that have not gone any further. I don't even have to ask why because I know. All of these women slept with him on the first date. I know it goes both ways, and that he is just as bad if he is having sex on the first date, but this is his rule, and he lives by it. There have been many times, before the first face to face meeting, that these women seem to have real potential. They have phone conversations, and email and text each other and seem very compatible. Then come the first date, the potential woman sleeps with him, and he doesn't contact her again. Many times, I wish that I could contact these women before the first date to tell them "Whatever you do, don't sleep with him on the first date. Or the second or third if you want a chance for this relationship to succeed." Then there are other times when I think, grown women should know this. I shouldn't have to tell anyone, in this day and age, to not sleep with someone on the first date. It just seems like common sense.

The thing about dating online is that it gets the nascent relationship on the wrong path from the get go. More than 65% of people who go online to find a date are looking for someone with whom they have a common interest and that the person is good looking.

When you combine that with the fact that most people use a friend to help write their profile, what you start to see is that the entire dating process is based on such superficial factors. And therein, as we have mentioned before, lies the problem.

The subconscious mind is not brought into the game until the initial selection has been made and the dating has begun. That's why the breakup rates are so high and the conversion rates, less than 20%, are so low. Conversely, out of all the people who are married today, only 5 % began as a date from an online portal.

Finding the right person to marry is simple if you bring the right arsenal to the meet. The main thing that is required is that you have to bring your developed subconscious mind into the game and reflect on what it has to tell you when you meet a person. You know that feeling you get sometimes when a person that you have met is just not right somehow, well that is the same corner of the mind that generates the approval and the possibility of compatibility.

Marriage needs to be based on your instincts which have been given sufficient information to make a pick. You can only do that with face to face encounters. There are so many nonverbal cues that a person puts out when they talk that your subconscious can't catch all of them when you are on a call, even if it's a video call. This is the main reason you need to meet in person. But the problem with online dating is that it can make people feel like their options are limitless. When you have too many options, you can at times become indecisive. Or you might always wonder if there is a better match out there for you. This is why online dating sometimes becomes more of a social attraction. For its social aspect. It's a great way to meet new people, but if you are tempted to continue to "shop" for more potential mates, you might miss the concept that relationships are based on. Commitment. It's hard to make a true commitment if your subscription doesn't expire for another two months.

Marriages are about commitment. Online dating is about social interaction and fun. If you are able to start with one objective and effectively transition, then you may be able to join that exclusive club of online daters who do indeed get married. I don't want to burst anyone's bubble because there are several people who have met their spouses online, but realistically, the odds can be against that. Therefore, it is very important to be clear in the beginning of what you are hoping to accomplish with online dating. Don't be afraid to express what it is that you are looking for. What have you got to lose? Nothing, but wasted time. I don't know about you, but I don't have time to waste.

13.
ONLINE DATING TESTIMONIES

Below you will find testimonies from those who have experienced online dating. We can learn a lot from other people and their experiences. Names have been changed for anonymity and privacy. When I asked for submissions I told the writers that they could write as much or as little as they wanted and that they could use detail and be honest because they would remain private. Therefore, a few of these are for adult eyes only. There is adult content within some of the testimonies below.

Testimony 1

I first thought about online dating when a friend recommended it to me. I had been single for a while and I wasn't having any luck with finding a partner. I wasn't sure at first. My first thought was no way! I am not going to put myself out there for everyone to see. I was frightened by the idea of it. Stranger danger came to mind. So, weeks passed and I continued to think about it. It was after coming home from a co-worker's wedding, that I decided to take the plunge into online dating. When the co-workers wedding invitation arrived in the mail addressed to 'Stephanie & Guest', I assumed that I'd be able to find a fun date for their big day. I wasn't able to, and I ended up going alone. I'm glad that I went, but I feel like it was that evening that helped me make the final decision that I didn't want this to happen again. Maybe if I had had a few potential online date options, this wouldn't have happened? I came home that evening, tore off my high heel shoes, poured myself a glass of wine and plumped down in front of my computer. I thought about a user name and finally decided on "Heaven Sent". That was taken so I had to think of a few more before I could even get started. Then came the self-description part. How would I describe myself? I instant messaged my best friend and asked for help. While I was waiting, I scrolled through some other profiles to get some ideas. I wanted it to sound really good and sophisticated. At first, I spent hours on the dating site. After some time, I realized that I needed to manage my time with it better. So, I'd log in and give myself 30 minutes to scan potential matches. I received a few emails from people who I could tell were not my type, so I'd politely tell them that I didn't think we'd be a good match. Most of the people seemed fine, but a few I could tell were mad about it. This was just confirmation to me that I had made the right decision. I went on a few dates, some of which were absolutely horrible. I will add that I always told someone where I was going and with who. I also made my date well aware that I had let someone know where I'd be. If a date suggested going someplace else, I'd say "Sure, but I need to text my change of plans to a friend, first." For the most part, everyone I went on a date with seemed nice enough, but unfortunately 'nice enough' just doesn't cut it. A few wanted to have sex on the first date which was a huge red flag for me, and I'd know not to see them again. One bragged about getting into fights. One guy had a child he never saw. One guy swore like a pirate. None of these things made me want to pursue the relationship further. Online dating was definitely trial and error. Eventually, after about a year of online dating, I did meet a great man whom I have been seeing for about two years now. It's been going really well and I am thankful to have met him. We have a lot in common, the sex is great, communication is good, and we are very compatible. It took time to let our guards down, and to take off the masks that we had learned to where for the outside world, but the more and more we become our authentic selves, the better our relationship gets. So for me, online dating eventually worked. I was about to give up several times, but I am glad that I didn't. ~ Mindy

Testimony 2

I became involved in a few very unhealthy relationships through online dating, and seemingly at the same time. I'm an executive woman in my 30's and I like dating men who have similar qualities and interests as me. The first guy I met online was the president of a banking firm. We met at a public restaurant and we had a lot of fun. There was definitely a physical attraction between us which is always a plus. He was a big, muscular guy with dark hair and brown eyes. He looked very Italian. We ended up going back to his place, which was over the top impressive. And because I don't have to use my real name with this, I will tell the truth. We ended up having sex. Rougher sex than I had ever had before, and I didn't know what to think about it. I left the next morning feeling a bit confused. What had just happened? The sex was a bit forceful but I didn't tell him to stop. I was sore and it was hard not to think about it throughout the day because every time I moved I was reminded of the night before. We had both agreed that we were going to continue to date others so that is what I did. The banker would call me when he wanted to hook up and most of the time I would accommodate. I'd go to his place, we'd have rough sex, and then I'd leave. After a few months, and him never asking me to do anything else, like meet his friends or family, I wondered if our relationship was going anywhere. I wanted to cuddle and get close after we had sex and he really didn't care to. Again, I found myself asking what I was doing? A woman my age should know better and I felt like I was being used and somewhat abused. I went on a few other first dates that didn't go any further because we just didn't click. One guy I met, we just couldn't even hold a conversation. It felt awkward and forced the whole time. When we ended the evening early, we thanked each other but didn't even politely say that we'd be in touch. That's how bad it was. We both knew that we would not be in touch again. The second guy who I dated regularly was nice enough. I didn't find him as attractive as the banker but he was nice and kind. After dinner, we walked to his car, and I let him kiss me and it was nice and gentle. He was sweet. Much different than the banker who would often grasp a whole handful of my hair and roughly pull my entire head back before swallowing my face. The second guy was a computer guy and seemed to have his stuff together. He didn't even try to have sex with me on the first date which was nice, indeed. I remember it was a Thursday night, and the banker called me and asked if I could meet him in an hour. I had plans with the computer guy, but for some reason I knew he would understand if I canceled. The banker guy told me to meet me at a tavern across from his condo and to wear something sexy. I did as I was told and wore a black dress that showed a lot of cleavage. We ordered an appetizer and a few drinks and he proceeded to tell me about his horrible day. He had to fire several of his favorite employees because they were downsizing and closing a few branches and he did not like to do that. These people had families they were supporting and although he knew it was a part of his job, he really loathed it. He was agitated and upset. He easily pulled me and my chair closer to him with one easy tug, and rested his hand in the slit of my dress. As he moved it up, he said,

"So, I'm really glad that you met me tonight. Because I need to think of something else for a while."

I replied, "What would you have done if I had had plans?"

He said, "Do you want me to be honest?"

"Yes, of course."

"I would've called someone else. Someone is always available." He leaned in and licked my neck.

His words stung, but his hand and tongue felt good.

To make a long story short, we ended up going back to his place. We had the roughest sex we had ever had and there was a part of me that was very scared. When he fell asleep, I gathered my clothes and quietly snuck out. I didn't even go to the bathroom which I remember I needed to do. I made the drive home and cried. A part of me wishing I wouldn't have canceled on computer guy. I knew how differently the night would've ended had I done that. When I got home, I realized I was bleeding in my private area, and the fear got worse. I remember thinking that I was glad that I had never told banker where I lived. I don't even know if he even knew my full name. The next day he texted me and asked where I went. I simply told him that I went home. He continued to text me from time to time asking if I could meet him, but I'd always give him a reason as to why I couldn't. Eventually, he stopped texting. I knew he would just contact someone else. As for the computer guy, I ended up marrying him and we now have a beautiful daughter. I guess if I were to give any advice about online dating, I would say to make sure you know who you are and exactly what you are looking for. If not, you can easily get confused and cross the line which will cause even more confusion. Know who you are. Respect yourself and your body, and don't do anything that you don't feel completely comfortable doing. I don't think I really knew who I was. I knew it didn't feel completely right, but I still didn't stop it from happening. I felt like a helpless child and I really wasn't! I had no self-respect, for my soul or my body. Thankfully, it all worked out okay. ~ Belinda

Testimony 3

I'm a 39-year-old male. I've been in two long-term relationships before, but never got married. One relationship lasted 7 years and the second lasted 9 years. That's 16 years of my life. I don't regret it because I learned a lot from it, but I would like another serious commitment. There is something about committed relationships that feel good to me. I know it's what I want. I've been on the online dating scene for about 2 years now. I wish all of the single women reading this, would take some advice. Stop being so easy. Yes, men are easy too, but isn't that just a given? I know not all men are slime balls, though. What I haven't come across yet, is a woman who is not easy. This is so disappointing to me. I've heard every excuse.

"Well if guys do it, women should be able to too." Really? Just because everyone else does it, doesn't mean you should too.

"It feels good, so why not do it on the first date? Really? Should I list why not?

"I was just testing you to see if you would sleep with someone on the first date." Oh, okay, that makes it better.

I do not want to continue to date someone if they will sleep with me on the first, second, or third date. Women tell me that I'm just as bad if I do it. I don't think so. If a woman wants to be easy, I'm not going to say no to that. I won't, however, want to go on a second date with her. I want a woman who honors and respects her body, not just someone who will sleep with any and every Tom, Dick, or Harry that comes along. I have yet to find the woman of my dreams with online dating. I don't want to give up and will leave it open as an option, but in all seriousness, the only thing I've found with online dating are quick screws. Yes, the women get mad at me when I don't want to see them again. I'm not a jerk, though. I will call and text back and tell them that I want to remain friends and try to explain how I feel about it. (What guy wouldn't want to stay friends with an easy woman?) Again, the most common response is "Well YOU did it." That's not the point. That point is, I'm not looking for a sleazy woman. Long-term I'm looking for a respectable one. ~ Rick

Testimony 4

I am a 29-year-old divorced male. I have met several nice ladies with online dating. I enjoy the ease of meeting people my age because I live in a small town which seems to be filled with the older generation. I work 50 hours a week, and find it difficult to meet women because of how much I work and where I live. Online dating is convenient because I can get a feel for the person before we meet up. There have been several women who I've communicated with online but decided not to meet because of differences we notice through emails or phone conversations. This helps save time. I only meet women who I feel I connect with because of our online or phone conversations. I try not to get my hopes up or let my expectations be too high. I've found that a lot of women tend to only put photos on that are either photoshopped or that make them look like model material. This just isn't reality, so there have been times when I hardly recognized the woman I was meeting. I had been looking at the pics she had downloaded, and she didn't look anything like it! I understand wanting to make your profile look and sound good, but I think the more realistic the better. My tip to women would be to be honest with your words and photos. You don't want someone to date you based on looks alone only anyway. The next tip I would give women is to not sleep with a man on the first date. I thought this was common knowledge but obviously, it isn't. So many women come on to me on the very first date. This may have been a turn on in high-school, or maybe even in the moment, but long-term it's the quickest turn off I've found. There is something about respecting yourself enough to wait. I've had to tell many women that I would not sleep with them on the first date. Most seem hurt and rejected when I do this. They don't seem to believe me, and then try harder to seduce me. Some have even stripped in front of me, and I've still remained steadfast as they give me a lap dance or through their cleavage in my face. I may not be the most gentlemanly guy out there, but sex on the first date is something that I won't do. I remember an article my mom shared with me when I was a teenager. It said that once you become one with another person, you will literally carry a piece of their aura with you for the rest of your life, so you need to be sure about who you are having intercourse with because it stays with you. I don't know if this has been a reason for my not wanting to have sex on the first date or not, but I honestly don't think so. I think the idea is just bad. It's such an intimate thing and I feel that I have more respect for woman than that. If I sleep with someone on the first date and then find out that they don't have a genuine and kind heart, then I will find myself in a mess, and someone will get hurt. I'm going to continue with online dating because it has been a good way for me to meet women I wouldn't ever get a chance to meet. I do hope that I will find someone long-term though. That is my goal. ~ Jerry

Testimony 5

I have experience with online dating and I am here to warn others about it. I am a 33-year-old independent woman with a good job. I started online dating about two years ago and didn't have much luck with it. Mostly it made me feel inferior and gave me lower self-esteem than I already had. I met a man online who I will call Bill. Bill emailed me first and asked if I would be interesting in meeting for coffee. He lived 30 minutes away from me. I told him that I'd rather get to know him a bit better online first, and he was okay with that. He told me that I could ask him anything. I liked that about him. He seemed witty and smart and the way he 'spoke' to me online was enchanting. He'd refer to me as 'Doll' or 'Sweetheart'. I found myself rushing home from work to see if I had an email from him. He told me he was an Operations Manager for a global corporation. He traveled a lot because of his job, but when I was ready he would love to take me out and spoil me. After a few months of communicating and answering questions back and forth online, I decided to face my fears and go for it. We met at a small coffee shop outside of town, and the minute I saw him I was somewhat hypnotized it seemed. I didn't know what hit me. His eyes maybe. Everything around me became blurred and I didn't even notice the waitress as she came to take our order. I couldn't speak so Bill ordered a coffee for me. He kept looking into my eyes and smiled the most sexiest smile ever. "Why have we waited this long to meet?" he asked. "Oh yes, you wanted to interview me and get to know me better first." he teased. We talked and laughed and when the waitress brought our coffee we both reached for the sugar jar at the same time. His hand rested on mine as I was about to pick it up, but he didn't move it away. He kept his hand on mine and looked again into my eyes. We were touching and the chemistry that was running between us was obvious. There was electricity in this one simple touch. When he finally pulled his hand away, he said, "You're as beautiful as your voice." We had an amazing first date and we definitely clicked. Something that doesn't happen often, in my experience. Bill called me whenever he could but he was hard to reach at times because of his job. When I realized that I could trust him, I let him pick me up at my place. He came in and looked around and said that he loved the place. My apartment was modern and I liked to keep it clean and simple. As I gave him a tour, he said that he liked my bedroom the most with a wink of the eye. My room was my sanctuary, and it did hold a romantic element to it. I am a hopeless romantic at heart and always have been. The next time Bill came over he brought flowers and ingredients so that he could cook me dinner. We made love that night and several times after that. It was amazing and I was on cloud nine. Bill had bought me a silk robe and as he slipped it over my naked body, I couldn't help but wonder how I got so lucky? Out of all the men online, I was the one to catch his eye. He made me breakfast in bed, and we made love in between bites of my delicious omelet. It was erotic in every sense of the word. He'd give me a bite, and then run a grape all over my body. He bit the grape in half and ran it down my neck, chest, navel, etc., and then he licked almost every inch of my body. He sat up in bed and I sat on top of him. As I slowly lowered myself down on him, he'd give me another bite and we would share it between our hungry mouths. Life was good. Bill and I dated for six months and I had yet to go to his place. I would, however, often meet him in the hotel rooms he'd have to stay in on business, many out of state. He'd buy me a plane ticket and I'd meet him there. One evening he met me at the airport and we had an hour drive to the hotel. I hadn't seen him in over two weeks, and it had seemed like an eternity. As I got off the plane and walked down the ramp, the anticipation welled up inside me. I wanted to push the people out of the way so that I could get to Bill. Hurry up people! When I finally reached the main airport, I stepped out into the lobby, and looked around. I didn't see Bill anywhere. I started to get nervous as I scanned the large area. Finally, I noticed him in the distance. He was leaning up against a back wall watching me. Adoration in his eyes. He was wearing a black jacket with jeans and he looked like he had just stepped out of a magazine. He was gorgeous. When I finally got to him, he told me that he just wanted to admire me. We embraced and the sexual tension was immediate. He smelled like he had just stepped out of the shower and I couldn't wait to get my hands on him. The sex between us had always been amazing. It was like we were the perfect fit. After we grabbed my luggage, we made way towards the parking lot. I was surprised when he led me to the shiniest car on the street. His business had hired him a limo to take him around the city. As the limousine driver opened the door for me, Bill put his hand on my waist to help guide me in and the electricity shot through me once me. I had hoped this feeling would never end. Bill did things to me in that limousine that had never been done to me before. And he did them in the sweetest way ever. Thankfully there was a private window between the driver and us. I felt so close to him. We had four days together. It was the longest time we had spent together in one span of time, because of his busy work schedule, and I was ready to savor it. On the second night, after an amazing evening of lovemaking, Bill's phone rang. He looked at it and said that he would have to take it outside on the balcony. I was spent so I just relaxed as I waited. I couldn't hear him that well but it seemed like a personal call. As I laid there, and ten minutes passed, I decided it might be fun to tease Bill while he was on the phone. He had done it to me a few times at my place when my mother had called. I'd try to hold a serious conversation as he was going down on me. Maybe I would do the same right now. I slipped my robe on and headed for the door. I slowly opened it, all I heard him say into the phone was "I love and miss you too, baby, and I can't wait to see you and the kids." I couldn't help but gasp out loud. Bill turned around with horror in his eyes. "I've got to go, baby. But I will call you back as soon as I can." He said as he hung up the phone. "Listen, I can explain." Bill said with fear in his eyes. He reached out to me and I yelled for him to explain. Bill was married. Not happily married according to him, although the conversation I heard him having with his WIFE would suggest differently! I was heartbroken and devastated and I wanted to get out of there as fast as I could. I was trying not to hyperventilate. Bill came up behind me and had the gall to say "Let's make love again, and then talk about this. I'm not happy with my wife, but you, you make me happy." How dare he? How did I not see the signs? Was I a mistress? I didn't want to be a mistress! How stupid can I be? How did this even happen! I grabbed my things and told Bill to never contact me again. I left the hotel and called my best friend crying. She had wondered why I hadn't met any of his family and friends yet. I thought it was just because he was busy. When the real reason was because he was married with a family! I thought I was going to puke. If there are ladies reading this, please do your homework before you let yourself fall for a guy. If you feel that something is off, it's probably because it is. Unfortunately, there are married men on these dating sites. It's unfortunate and not okay. They prey on trusting women and use their words to manipulate. It took me a long time to get over Bill. My heart still hurts thinking about it. I'm not saying that all men do this, and I know that there are married women on these sites as well. All I'm saying is to be sure you do your homework well in advance before you start to let your emotions get involved. I thought I was doing that by waiting to meet Bill until he had answered several questions and until we had established an online relationship that seemed to be a good mix. Now that I think back, I did ignore a lot of red flags. Like the fact that I had never been to his place, and that he traveled out of town a lot, and that he was always 'working', therefore, I had to always wait for him to contact me. Red flags that I ignored because I was blinded. For me online dating didn't work, but I know it has for others. I've been burned though, so I think I'm just going to wait to meet someone in real life instead of online. I actually have a date scheduled for next week with a guy I went to high school with. I know him and his family and I'm looking forward to a familiar date. We seem to like the same things and I'm excited to see him. ~ Jenny

Testimony 6

I am a 21-year-old male who attends college fulltime. My goal is to become a doctor like my father, therefore, I don't have time for a serious relationship, but I still like to go out from time to time. Online dating has worked in that regard. I have met a lot of women this way. Everyone is so different and I respect that about human beings. I do not judge people for their beliefs or for their likes or dislikes. Everyone has different preferences and to each his own is a motto I like to live by. You see a lot of diversity in the online world of dating and you must know what you want in order to succeed. I know what I want right now. I want to date and have fun in the little time that I can commit to it. Most of my time is scheduled for classes and studying. Some of the pros and cons of online dating would have to be those who don't truly know who they are or what they want. I've met several women who said they agreed with me and that they, too, did not want anything serious. I am always honest right from the get go with the women I meet. Honesty is a value that I take very seriously. So, I've had several women say that they totally accept and respect my request to not be serious only to have them change their minds after just a few dates. One women started stalking me after I told her that I felt that we were getting too serious. I could tell that she was starting to expect me to see her. I felt that it was starting down an unhealthy path, and I reminded her of our agreement when we starting hanging out. I didn't want to hurt her. She got mad and started following me. It seemed like every place I went; she would just happen to show up shortly afterwards. I knew she must be following me. When she started to befriend my roommates, I knew I was in trouble. I tried to tell her politely that we needed to stop seeing each other. I could tell that she wanted more than I could give. One night, after an evening out at the club, she and a friend of hers showed up with my roommate. I said hi, but told everyone that I was going to bed because I had to get up early for class. I shut out the light and got into bed. I could hear them talking and laughing outside my door. The next thing I knew, my roommate opened the door and pushed her in. I was thinking that I was going to kill him the next morning. He later told me that she just wouldn't stop talking about me, so he didn't know what else to do. She landed on my bed and I asked what she was doing. Here I was naked under the covers with a woman who wouldn't stop stalking me. I had tried to be polite and respectful. We had only dated for about a month but we had had sex at least a handful of times, and although it was great, I still didn't feel comfortable with how serious she was getting. I couldn't handle serious right then. There was no way with my studies and work load. I had a goal and a scholarship that depended on my getting good grades. I couldn't blow it. As she laid down beside me, she said "I'm sorry if you're trying to sleep. I just can't seem to get enough of you." She started to kiss my neck and rub my back. I didn't want to be a complete jerk and ignore her, but I didn't want to lead her on either. I was laying on my back and she was giving me a light massage. She smelled good and she was a very attractive girl. Her hands went lower and lower until she was massaging my ass. It felt good and I could feel myself getting aroused. When she reached down between my legs and lightly tickled my testicles, I knew I should stop her, but in the moment, I didn't know why I should. We were both single, she knew I didn't want anything serious, and we were in my dark bedroom. She rolled me over and headed down under the blankets. She started sucking on me and there was no going back. After she left, I went to sleep knowing that wasn't the best decision I had ever made, but she was a grown woman. She continued with this behavior for weeks. She'd see me out at the club and just stare at me while I danced with other women. I'd try to move to a different side of the club, but she'd follow and watch me. I finally had to pull her aside and tell her that she was acting desperate. I could not continue to date her because she was taking it too serious. She kept hoping that I would change my mind, but I kept telling her that I wasn't going to. Finally, I had to stop going out for a while. I'd take my dates elsewhere where she couldn't find me. Eventually we lost touch, but that is the biggest con I've found with online dating. The women say they don't want to be serious, but after a few dates, they seem to want me to make a commitment to them. It's difficult so I try to be very clear right from the start. So, to recap, cons are people who aren't who they say they are or who want something different than they say they do. Pros are that you can meet a lot of people and have many options for dates. I will continue to participate in online dating. ~ Trent

Testimony 7

I think I tried every single dating site that is out there over a span of three years. Yes, three years. To some this may not seem like a long time, but for me, it felt like an eternity. I just got more and more frustrated with each one. And in all honestly, I felt less and less worthy as well. I felt like more than half of the men just wanted younger women. Many of the men who I felt would be compatible were looking for women 10 to 15 years younger than them! When I'd come across a man who was looking for someone his own age, it felt like a rarity! I'd wink at someone or click that I was interested only to receive no feedback. It was hard not to take it personal. What's wrong with me? That was a question I asked myself often. I started questioning everything. Was my profile too long or not long enough? Did I sound too serious in it? Did I not answer the questions correctly? I did go on several dates where I would meet the man usually half way between our two hometowns. Some men insisted on paying the bill, others agreed to going in half. I met one man who was not clean. He didn't look anything like his profile photo. He smelled like he hadn't showered in a week, and I barely got through my coffee and muffin. I tried not to be impolite, but I tend to be on the honest side, so I just thanked him for his time and told him that I just didn't think we were going to work out. One guy, who I thought I could really connect with, told me that he wants to date and sleep with many women, so I wouldn't be the only one. Yes he wanted to sleep with me that night, but he was honest and said he'd be planning on sleeping with another woman the very next night! I guess I should have thanked him for his honesty, but I wondered why he didn't tell me this before I drove 45 minutes to meet him. It was a waste of time and again, a little piece of my heart hurt because of it. Again, I felt not good enough. It's hard not to take any kind of rejection personal, and it seems like there is a lot of rejection with online dating. I guess I could usually always tell within the first 10 minutes. Maybe that is shallow of me, but it seems to be how it worked for me. I dated at least a couple dozen men over three years and like I said I tried every single dating site I could find. I paid a lot in membership fees, and had decided that the last site I had subscribed to would be my last. Not only because it was the last dating site that I knew of, but because I had had enough. I was giving up on the online dating thing. It just wasn't for me, and each night that I logged in without any activity, the more discouraged I got. What is wrong with me? In the outside world, people seem to really like me, so why was this online thing not working? I had one week left of my membership. One week. And I was rarely checking it anymore because there was rarely anything worth checking. This was at the same time that I was doing a fast for God. The last few years I have been growing my relationship with the Lord and really trying to obey his commandments. Do not lie, cheat, steal, gossip, get drunk, envy, judge, but forgive and love everyone, etc. This is taking me a lot of practice but my mind and heart is being transformed and renewed. So, I decided to take my loyalty one step further for God, and I decided to cut out something for 40 days that I knew would NOT be easy. And it wasn't easy. The first 3 weeks were the most difficult but I did it. On the last week of my fast, I received an email from a new member on the online dating site. And he lived in my town! He lived 5 minutes away from me! We met at a local restaurant and we laughed for 3 hours straight almost. We connected and hit it off splendidly. We have been dating for almost a year now and he even moved in with me. We are such a great match and I am so grateful that I met him. I can't imagine now not knowing him. I am very much in love and I am not afraid to say so.

~Sara

Testimony 8

I was a 23-year-old virgin when I began online dating. I believe in the Bible and in purity, therefore, I subscribed to a few online Christian dating sites. The characteristics between the men who are truly respectable are so different from the characteristics of men who have not been taught how to be respectable and many of those men are only after one thing. Again, because they haven't been taught or because they haven't had good role models. I recently went out to eat and there was a table of two older men. They were clearly checking my friend and I out from head to toe. They were googling over our backsides as we walked by and one even whistled. This is very different from the men I know who are respectable. I also recently went to a movie with a group of people who live the Christian values. During the movie, there were two scenes that showed a woman in her bikini. Out of the cover of my eye, I looked over at one of the guys in the group. He is a young, good looking guy, who is also a musician. I was surprised to notice that during both bikini scenes, he looked away from the screen. What a difference between the men I had encountered in the restaurant. Although I am young, I had had enough experience to observe the drastic details. Some of the guys I went to college with, before they knew who I was in my soul, would text me asking if I'd send them nudes pictures. I was horrified at first. But I decided to text back with a short and polite message saying that I had no interest in doing that, and they obviously didn't know me as well as they thought they had. I am well aware of the differences in character of true Christian men and those who have only dabbled in the word, therefore, I assumed some of these Christian dating sites would be perfect for me. Although I consider myself to be smart enough, I also know that I was very vulnerable at times. I like to believe the best in people. The first few men that I met, didn't really seem to be Christians. They claimed to be, but they didn't attend church or anything like it. I like to go to church every Sunday, to recharge my battery and to learn more. There is always so much to learn. I didn't always go to church, and as a matter of fact, I knew nothing about the Bible or God until my teenage years when I went to a youth group meeting with a friend. Although I didn't know anything about God or the Bible, I remember when I was around 11 years old, I was sitting outside and I sensed the presence of the Divine Source. I knew that there was something that was aware of me, and that cared for me. I sensed an open communication with this Diving Being. Throughout my high school years, I felt this presence pursuing me in a sense; calling me closer. So, I decided to do some research. I learned more than just the ten commandments, which are amazing in of themselves. But I also learned that the Bible says that we shouldn't drink to get drunk, and that we need to forgive others over and over again, until they have a change of heart. I learned that we are to give thanks in all circumstances, and that we are not supposed to complain or gossip. Jealously and envy are also sins. The key is to love and accept one another without judgement. I learned that we are to pray without ceasing. I learned so much! And my life started to change for the better! I was being transformed, and everything in my life was striving because of it. Everything except for my online dating endeavor. The first guy I met through a Christian online dating website told me that he had slept with several women and that he felt that having sex is the best way to see if a couple is truly compatible. I asked how many women he had slept with, and he didn't want to tell me. I asked if he could at least tell me if it was more than 20. Had he slept with more than 20 women in his lifetime. He didn't hesitate to answer with an affirmative yes. He told me he thought we should "do it" and see how we "fit". I told him I was a virgin, and he seemed shocked. I can't imagine how many women he had slept with, but if that is how he measures compatibility, and he hadn't found the one yet, I didn't think his method is a very good one. Although I knew about his past, he was sweet and he knew how to make me feel good about myself. He showered me with compliments and gifts. I couldn't help but wonder, deep down inside, if I was just a challenge for him, being a virgin and all, but I let that negative thought dissipate as soon as it entered my brain. He was charming. His name was Sean and he was tall, muscular, and handsome. He was in a football league and I could clearly see that he worked out daily. He was very polite, and on our fifth date he arranged a beautiful picnic for the two of us in a beautiful park by the water. He brought wine, flowers, and chocolates. As he opened my car door and escorted me to the blanket he had laid out, I couldn't help but notice his gorgeous eyes shining in the sun. His dirty blond hair was thick and had a bit of a natural curl to it. He was wearing cargo shorts and a collared shirt. He told me that I looked beautiful and kissed me on the cheek. As we sat on the blanket, and got comfortable, he poured me a glass of wine. He had strawberries and cheese all prepared. It was a glorious day and I felt amazing. I wore a sundress and sandals. As he started to feed me the strawberries, I couldn't help but feel smitten with him. What a nice thing for him to do. Sean moved closer and fed me another strawberry. He started kissing me and licking the strawberry flavor from my lips. It felt good. He was a good kisser. Sean had brought a real estate magazine he wanted to show me. As I grabbed it and laid flat on my tummy, getting ready to open it, he did the same but was partial laying on top of me, while looking over my shoulder. He steadied himself over me and moved his hands over mine to guide me to the correct page. He was looking at buying a house and he wanted me to see it. As he flipped through the pages he was now laying directly on my backside, and I could feel his breath on my neck. He was very excited to show me his dream home. He was thinking about making an offer on it. When we got to the page, he showed me the house and told me all about it. It was a cute house with an attached garage and a huge yard. I told him I loved it and could totally see him in it. He started kissing my neck and ear. Reaching my mouth, he moved his tongue all around mine and I could feel his erection on my back. He started rubbing the hem of my dress and I let him. It felt nice. His bare hands on my legs. He told me that he could lift my dress up and push himself inside me right then and there without anyone knowing what was happening. There weren't too many people around as it was early afternoon, and he had an extra blanket on top of us. I reminded him that I was a virgin and that not only did I not want to lose my virginity this way, but that I was planning on waiting until I got married. Sean stopped in his tracks and told me that he had no desire to get married anytime soon. He just wanted to know if we would be compatible. I thought we were compatible. We laughed and played well together. We could carry on an intelligent conversation. We ate the cheese and crackers in silence and ended the evening without really committing to seeing each other again. I didn't know what to expect. I was sad because I missed talking with him. About a week later, Sean called and we continued dating for another three months. I met a lot of his friends and he met a lot of mine. I was starting to question my belief system. Did I want to wait? Maybe I didn't really need to wait. I was clearly falling in love with this amazing man. On our 4 month 'anniversary' he asked if I could meet him at the pier that Saturday. He had rented a sailboat! It was an amazing adventure. We sailed for hours and it was exciting and exhilarating. The wind in our hair, the fast pace of the wild ocean as we cruised along. We ended up slowing down and decided to put the anchor down and enjoy a late lunch. We went down under where there was a small restroom, table, and bed. I was wearing a pair of elastic waisted shorts with a tank top, and Sean was only wearing his swim suit. We ate lunch and drank wine. We started kissing and touching each other. Sean reached for the bottom of my tank top and when he lifted it up over my head, I couldn't believe I was actually letting him. Sean looked at my breasts and then looked into my eyes, "I love you" he said. I felt confused. I felt desperately in love with him, but our beliefs were different. For years, I had been strong and adamant about holding onto my faith. The Bible clearly says that you should not have sex before marriage and for good reason. Nothing good can come from sex before marriage. Sean picked up his glass of wine and slowly poured some of it over my nipples before slowly lowering his head to suck it off. I felt like I was in heaven. The wine was cold but his mouth was hot. I felt myself laying back and surprised myself when I heard a moan escape from my mouth. But I wanted this type of thing to happen on my wedding night, not with some guy who may not stick around. As his tongue swirled around each of my nipples, my thoughts swirled inside my head. What is happening? I wanted it so bad, and I knew that the enemy would have a party if I gave my virginity to this man right here and now. I sat up and stopped Sean from what he was doing. As I pushed him away, my nipple was still in his mouth; the pull and release felt good and I could feel it throbbing. "I just want to feel you," he said. "I want to see if we are as sexually compatible as I think we will be. I want you so badly. I love you and there is nothing I want more right now."

"Sean, I told you the day we met, that I was a virgin and that I was going to wait until marriage."

"Yes, but we are in love. Doesn't that change things?"

"No, it shouldn't."

Sean was clearly frustrated with me, but we managed to have a good rest of the evening and we didn't mention it again for a few more weeks. On the day, he got the keys to his new house, he called me extremely excited. We had been packing up his apartment for weeks. He had movers helping him and he hoped I could come over to a little house warming dinner he had planned with a few friends. Of course, I wouldn't miss it. The house was amazing, and the dinner was fun. His friends were all wonderful people. After everyone left, Sean asked if I'd spend the first night in his new house with him. He said there was no one else he would want to share such a special moment with. I thought about it and struggled with making the decision. I loved this sexy, thoughtful man. I told him that I would spend the night as long as he didn't expect to have sex. "Of course not," he said. As I picked up the kitchen, he went in his bedroom, and unpacked a few more things. When we were done, Sean put some music on the stereo and we danced in his living room. We kissed and I could feel his erection grow between us, but I trusted that he wouldn't push it. He knew how I felt. It was such a romantic night and I was so happy to be there with him. When we walked into his bedroom, I realized that he had lit some candles and it looked amazing. I couldn't help but wish that this was my wedding night. We crawled into Sean's bed in his new room, and we were both so excited and giddy. He was a homeowner! We kissed and hugged and unfortunately the night was slightly ruined because Sean expected me to change my mind. I was so frustrated because he wasn't respecting my wishes at all. He kept thinking that I should change my belief system and I almost did several times, but I kept reminding myself to be strong. To not lose sight of my goal. Sean told me that night that he didn't think he would ever be ready to get married, and I could feel my heart breaking. We broke it off because obviously, he wasn't willing to wait and I wasn't about to throw away my virginity and beliefs for someone who didn't know what he wanted. It was one of the hardest times I've ever been through. I probably shouldn't have let things go as far as I did, but because I did, our emotions became even more twisted. It has been proven that being romantically involved in any physical way (it doesn't have to be actual sex; it can be any physical closeness) causes a bond of sorts. Chemicals get released in your brain that cause a bond which then causes breakups to be even more heartbreaking. I shouldn't have been so dumb. I'm not trying to beat myself up, but I should have known better. Online dating didn't work for me, but I eventually met a wonderful guy at church. We dated for 6 months, and got married. We've been married for 3 years now and are going strong. I am so glad that I waited. My marriage is amazing in every way. ~ Alisha

Testimony 9

My husband and I met through an online dating site and I am very thankful that I didn't give up because I felt like giving up many times. Dating several people can be really stressful. I think the difference between online dating and dating in the real world, per say, is that you will have many more options with online dating. You could arrange four dates in a week with online dating, but in the real world that isn't very realistic. You'd probably only get four dates a month and that's if you're lucky. Dating is stressful and can take a toll mentally and emotionally. At least for me, it did. Dating stressed me out. I had several dates with men that I didn't want to see again for one reason or another, or they didn't want to see me again. That was tough. Rejection takes on a whole new level and the odds for rejection are a lot higher with online dating. You have to really try not to get upset if someone doesn't want to see you again. You have to remember that the odds are low of you finding your perfect match right off the bat. Of course, there really isn't a perfect match, but you know what I mean. Chances of you finding a good match right off, are slim, so keep at it, and don't take anything personal. If someone doesn't want to see you again, trust that they are not the one for you, and move on. My husband and I are so happy that we found each other. We have been married for 7 years now and we are still going strong. But we have plenty of entertaining stories about the online dating period of our lives. He said that he dated several women who were very different. One was planning their wedding on the 3rd date! That's moving fast I'd say. He told her that he thought proposals were needed to plan a wedding. We joke that we are glad that he didn't end up marrying her. If you don't take anything personal, and know that online dating can take some time, you will be all set. There are many people out there in the world, and with online dating, you will have access to many of them. I wish you the same luck that I had, if that is what you are looking for. ~ Lisa

Testimony 10

My experience with online dating. I met the most amazing man online. It's an amazing story and I love sharing it, so when you asked for submissions, I jumped at the chance. Thank you! We met on an online dating website. All I knew was that he lived within 20 miles from me, and that his user name was naturevsnuture. And that is all he knew about me as well. With the exception of our profile descriptions which described a few of our hobbies, etc. For about four months we emailed each other without even knowing each other's first names. We just referred to each other by our usernames. We had great online rapport and I truly enjoyed communicating with him. He was intelligent and had a great sense of humor. For four months, we emailed each other almost daily. It was exciting and fun and I could feel that we truly had a connection. He told me that he thought about me all day long, and I told him I couldn't wait to meet him in person. After four month of communicating daily, I felt close to him. I felt the urge to hug and kiss him. I couldn't believe I felt this way and I hadn't even met him in person yet, but it felt real. I wanted to kiss this man. The man who I was learning to confide in. The man who made my days brighter. We started calling each other and talking on the phone almost nightly. Naturevsnurture finally told me that he was a doctor and I couldn't help but wonder if I knew him. I had previously worked at large medical facility in the area, as a traveling assistant, and I knew most of the doctors there, but his voice didn't sound familiar. I also knew that there were a lot of hospitals and clinics in the area so the chances were low. I found that we were expressing our deepest fears and secrets in email and by doing so we were growing closer and closer. I valued his opinion and he always had a way of making me feel better about life. He told me what he wanted to do to me. He said he wanted to take me in his arms and protect me. He wanted to look into my eyes and kiss me until the thoughts and stresses of the day melted away. He said he hoped that we got along this well in person. He believed that we would because of how easy and effortless our online and phone communication had been. We decided to meet on a walking trail in the area. He told me to look for a black truck and that he would meet me there. My first thought was of a doctor I once knew of. A doctor I had never met but knew owned a black truck. There was a doctor who I saw often at the lab I traveled to, and we often made eye contact that lasted longer than usual, I felt something in his eyes, but we had never talked or been introduced. I saw this doctor often in the halls, at meetings, and I witnessed him saving lives. He was a hero in my eyes. There was one time when we were at a large convention and a man in a wheelchair feel off a small ramp. He was the only one to run up and help the man out. I was impressed and in awe of him. Somehow, over time because we worked together, I knew what he drove, and he knew what I drove, and for years we would actually wave to each other when we passed each other on the street. Although I was completely attracted to this doctor, the time was never right I guess. I always felt intimidated by his good looks and confident stride. I always got nervous when he was around. I even got nervous when I waved to him in passing. I often imagined what I would say if I ever got the opportunity. Would this be my opportunity? Although the thought quickly crossed my mind, I didn't think it could be the same doctor. I arrived in the parking lot 10 minutes early. I was nervous and excited to meet this man. I felt as though I cared for him already. For over five months we had been sharing our thoughts and feelings with each other and to say that I was anxious would have been an understatement. I checked myself in the mirror. We were planning on walking along a public beach and there was a beautifully landscaped path with picnic tables and wooded areas with swings and grass. When he pulled in, I recognized his black truck right away. It was him! He pulled up beside me and we were both in disbelief. I was so nervous. What was I going to say? I hoped it wouldn't be awkward and uncomfortable. At least I knew him fairly well now so I'd have things to talk about. As I jumped out of my vehicle, he met me at my door. "I can't believe it's you." He said giving me a hug. "But I'm glad that it is. You're not a stranger after all." We stayed in each other's arms as he looked at me. I was speechless. "I don't know what to say", I managed to squeak out.

"Well what do you think?" he asked.

"I think I've known you for years, but I haven't known you. I know you. I've seen you. I've admired you. I know you." I was blabbering and not making much sense.

"Yes we know each other," he grabbed my hands, "I've seen you before. I've really seen you, in all your mystery and I'm excited that we are here, together, now. I asked about you years ago."

"You asked about me?" I asked curiously.

"Yes, but then I didn't see you again. Except driving in town from time to time." He put his hand in my hair and looked into my eyes. "I know you, so can I kiss you? I have, to be honest, I've wanted to kiss you for a long, lonnnng time." His voice was low and sexy.

"Yes, please. Me too." I still wasn't making sense.

NaturevsNuture leaned in close and started slowly placing light kisses on my lips. It was amazing and good and I felt like I was in a dream. As we strolled along, giggling, we held hands and kept taking turns saying "Hey, I know you." Because I knew him, I now felt completely safe with him. We dated for a few more months and couldn't believe how well we got along. And then one night we finally went back to his place. We drank wine and made love for hours. Afterward we jumped in the shower and washed each other's bodies and made love again as the hot water poured down over us. I didn't know how this was happening. The man I had watched from a distance for so long. The man I made eye contact with years ago, the man I never thought I would get a chance to talk to. The man I admired for his strength, courage, confidence, decisiveness, drive, charm, and loyalty. He was the definition of a man, and as he pulled me into bed again, I was happy to be with him and to be laying in his arms feeling the warmth of his body against mine. As he kissed my neck, cheeks, nose, chin, each eye, forehead, and lips, he looked at me and said, "I think this is going to be really good. I have a really, really good feeling about this." We have been dating ever since and things couldn't be better. I am so in love with this man, and I still can't believe how the Universe brought us together. ~ Melanie

CONCLUSION

In the final analysis, if your objective is to get married, then online dating can work, but might not be the most efficient way to go about it. If you do find your mate via online dating, then you need to make sure that you don't hold their past there against them and that they do the same for you. Online dating is a modern way of meeting people.

If you do find someone you want to become serious with, making the decision to unsubscribe and end your memberships to the online dating sites, and to commit to one another, if that is the ultimate goal, is the largest part of staying together. Commitment is what a committed relationship (and marriage) is about - it doesn't matter where you meet or how you meet.

Online dating carries with it certain risks that you must understand and until you are able and confident that you can mitigate those risks, only then should you step into it. Getting onto other social media can be less dangerous because there is less chance of a real life rendezvous, unlike online dating where the whole point is to eventually meet up.

That being the case, the industry for online dating is not shrinking. On the contrary, it is growing at a steady pace. It is especially popular in the United States with young adults in the mid-20s to late 30 and it even extends to those in their 60s and 70s.

There are different online dating sites and they are not limited to plain vanilla dating, nor are they limited to the United States. There are dating sites specializing in almost every corner of the world. But be extremely wary because a number of these foreign sites have two kinds of participants. One is a major cover-up operation for escorts. The others are often looking for husbands in the United States, mainly so that they can immigrate there. Being aware and on the lookout for red flags can help save you from trouble and heartbreak.

If you do decide to try online dating, then make sure you understand that the other person's intentions may not mirror your own. It is not considered impolite to ask their intentions early in the game to avoid disappointment from the start.

For adults, online dating can be an extremely invigorating pastime or it can be a social avenue to advance one's network. Whatever your objective, whatever your decision, make it clear to the other person, that way everyone knows exactly what to expect, going in.

Finally, do not part with money if someone you meet through an online dating site asks you for some. Be it a loan or a gift, stay far away from mixing money with this social engagement. If the subject of money comes up, it is a red flag that you should not overlook, but take heed and move on.

Regardless of how you view online dating, make sure you never reveal private information to strangers on these sites. Two things can happen. First, your potential date, whom you have yet to properly meet poses a risk of stalking or blackmailing you.

The second thing that you don't want to see happen is for some cyber bully to get ahold of your information because then you could have to deal with identity theft and possible harassment. Never provide your home address online until and unless you are totally comfortable with the person.

If you can, arrange double dates with the person you are meeting for the first time, that way you get to see the person in action, you will get to see how they respond to you and your friends and you will get to see him or her in a more relaxed setting.

Finally, never send compromising pictures of yourself when you meet someone via online dating. And be sure that it is a major red flag if the person asks you for to do so. Nothing you send online is private.

Online dating is not for everyone. Again, trust your instincts. Don't be pushed into it. If you feel you want to give it a try, go ahead but stay true to yourself. You can exit the scene, at any time, and increase your social life outdoors with various activities that you research. Often times if people spent as much time socializing at local events, gatherings, church, etc., as they did on dating sites, they would have a good chance of meeting a potential mate in the real world.

What Now?

Well, now you've learned the ins and outs of online dating.

You have received dating etiquette advice, have a good idea which sites may be good options for you, you know how to approach building a profile and using the sites, and you have much of the information you will need to protect yourself. If you have read this and decided that online dating isn't for you, we hope it was at least interesting and educational. But what if you are ready to get out there and start dating?

The only thing left to do now is to decide if online dating is right for you! If it is, choose a site or two and put yourself out there. If you find someone you would really like to meet, make sure you take the precautions we listed, whether you are a male or a female. Use our etiquette tips, and remember it takes time to nurture a real relationship no matter where you meet.

I Met Someone! What do I Tell People?

Tell them you met your new mate online, of course! As we mentioned in our introduction, we aren't living in the stone age anymore – most people aren't going to have a stigma about online dating. We hope you enjoyed this book on online dating, whether you decide it is for you or not!

ABOUT SAGE WILCOX

Sage lives in the United States with her husband, children, cat, and dog. She is a certified energy healer. Sage enjoys giving advice to her clients, friends, and family on healing, love, and relationships. She also enjoys studying human behavior, reading, writing, being outdoors, and enhancing her relationships with others. She enjoys reading and learning the Bible. In her experience, the more she learns and practices the Word, the better her life becomes.

Other books by Sage Wilcox:

- *Love Letters from Exes: Proof That Life Goes On After a Break Up and Love Is What You Make It*

- *Get It Up: 101 Ways to Raise Your Vibration, Reduce Stress, Depression, & Anxiety, Increase Joy, Peace, & Happiness and Attract Abundance Automatically!*

- *The 2-Hour Vacation: Let Go and Relax, Reduce Stress & Anxiety, Gain Inner Peace, and Happiness*

- *Until We Fall (A Romance Novel)*

- *The Importance of Doing It: How to Utilize Discipline to Get Out of Bed, and Make Your Dreams Come True! A Guide to Taking Action to Create Successful Habits, Reduce Stress, Anxiety, & Depression & Gain Self-Discipline, Motivation, & Success!*

- *Less Is Best: Declutter, Organize, & Simplify to Reach Minimalism; Get More Time, Money, & Energy*

Please visit her at:
http://sagewilcox.wix.com/books
www.facebook.com/sagewilcoxbooks
Thank you!

Disclaimer

The purpose of this book is for entertainment purposes only. This book is designed to provide information and motivation to our readers. The content of each article, letter, or insight is the sole expression and opinion of its author, and not necessarily that of the publisher. The letters contained in this book are from contributors and are the contributor's recollections of their experiences. This is a work based on opinions, recollections, and true events, however, names, characters, businesses, places, and incidents are either the products of the authors' imaginations or used in a fictitious manner. Any resemblance to actual persons, living or dead, businesses, companies, events, locales, or actual events is entirely coincidental. This book is not intended nor is it implied to be a substitute for professional medical advice, and any medical advice and any medical information contained in this book is not intended to be diagnostic or treatment in any way. The author and publisher are not engaged in rendering medical, psychological, legal, or any other professional services. If medical, psychological or other expert assistance is required, please talk to your physician and locate the services of a competent professional. The author and publisher shall have neither liability nor responsibility to any person or entity with respect to any loss or damage caused, or alleged to have been caused, directly or indirectly, by the information contained in this book. Neither the publisher nor the individual author(s) shall be liable for any physical, psychological, emotional, financial, or commercial damages, including, but not limited to, special, incidental, consequential or other damages. Our views and rights are the same: You are responsible for your own choices, actions, and results. If you do not wish to be bound by the above, you may return this book along with a copy of the receipt to the publisher for a full refund.

www.ingramcontent.com/pod-product-compliance
Lightning Source LLC
Chambersburg PA
CBHW060946040426
42445CB00011B/1023